Routledge Revivals

Capital, Inflation and the Multinationals

Inflation is the economic plague of the modern world, completely undermining conventional theory and policies for its containment, and setting governments, management and labour on a dangerous collision course. Its alarming spread is only paralleled by the expansion of multinational corporations, some of them more economically powerful than nation states. This book, first published in 1971, provided a totally new perspective on these phenomena, linking them in a common theory based on a thorough analysis of the modern role of capital financing in the global economy. It demonstrates the impact of technology on self-financing growth and explains why inflation can never be stemmed by attacks on wage costs when the source lies in the need of managements to maximise cash flows. Alternative economic policies are discussed, including proposals for creating assets for workers in the self-financing investment. Charles Levinson draws together the strands of his subject in a way which is comprehensive and rigorous, yet easily accessible to the more general reader. The conclusions reached in *Capital Inflation and the Multinationals* are still of great interest and relevance to professional economists and students, political practitioners and commentators.

Capital, Inflation and the Multinationals

Charles Levinson

Routledge
Taylor & Francis Group

First published in 1971
by George Allen & Unwin Ltd

This edition first published in 2013 by Routledge
2 Park Square, Milton Park, Abingdon, Oxon, OX14 4RN

Simultaneously published in the USA and Canada
by Routledge
711 Third Avenue, New York, NY 10017

Routledge is an imprint of the Taylor & Francis Group, an informa business

Publisher's Note

The publisher has gone to great lengths to ensure the quality of this reprint but points out that some imperfections in the original copies may be apparent.

Disclaimer

The publisher has made every effort to trace copyright holders and welcomes correspondence from those they have been unable to contact.

A Library of Congress record exists under LC control number: 71872014

ISBN 13: 978-0-415-82923-6 (hbk)
ISBN 13: 978-0-203-51532-7 (ebk)

CAPITAL, INFLATION AND THE MULTINATIONALS

by

CHARLES LEVINSON

London
GEORGE ALLEN & UNWIN LTD
RUSKIN HOUSE MUSEUM STREET

FIRST PUBLISHED IN 1971

ISBN 0 04 330196 7 CASED
0 04 330197 5 PAPER

PRINTED IN GREAT BRITAIN
in 11 on 12 pt Times Roman
BY CPI ANTONY ROWE
CHIPPENHAM AND EASTBOURNE

Contents

1. Introduction

Inflation is now proclaimed the critical problem of industrial society, and probably will become its obsession. This applies not only to the market economies of the West, but to the controlled economies of the East and to industrialized as well as to developing countries. Forecasts are almost without exception for sustained or increasing rates of price rises in the years ahead. The atmosphere is best described as glum and nervous.

The persistent rise in prices is occurring, contrary to all past experience, in circumstances which had been considered inimical to their growth: economic stagnation, deflationary fiscal and monetary policies, comparatively high levels of unemployment. Even the foreign trade balances of many countries have been behaving in a strange, eccentric way. In 1970 they have been impressively stronger for most countries, including the chronic sufferers such as the UK, USA or France, despite inflation.

EXPERT OPINION

Professor Paul A. Samuelson
Newsweek, February 1971

'Creeping inflation is the malaria of the modern mixed economy. Like malaria it is uncomfortable to live with and just will not go away. But unlike the case of malaria, there seems to be no known cure for creeping inflation that is better than the disease.'

All in all it has been a very bad period for professional economists and forecasters. The phenomenon of 'stagflation', a situation in which prices have risen together with stagnation and unemployment, was not picked up on any of the economic antennae, nor foreshadowed in the print-outs of the proliferating computerized econometric models. It has been even more discomforting for the policy-makers and political pundits. Inflation is not responding to recession and unemployment; investments continue to rise despite historic highs in interest rates; wage rises in the areas of 10% to 15% have not automatically led to comparable rises in unit labour costs, or to greater consumer demand.

YESTERDAY'S WISDOM IS TODAY'S NONSENSE

There still persists, of course, a widespread and strident chorus of conventionalism which continues to see the wages–prices relationship as the unique cause of the dilemma, and the application of demand management and incomes policies as the remedy. This thinking still sees inflation as a cost-push or demand-pull process in which excessive average wage increases, relative to the improvement in annual labour productivity, produce pressure on prices. This reasoning accepts as an article of faith that price adjustments are automatic responses to abnormally compressed profit margins or too much consumer money chasing too few goods.

Whatever the variations in given situations, the basis of any incomes policy is to control and maintain wage rises within some selected range considered compatible with a moderately rising level of prices and full employment. The simultaneous application of controls to other forms of unearned income, such as dividends, interest, etc., and the pegging of retail prices, seek merely to create the appearance of equality and fairness. In practice, however, it is virtually impossible to control the non-wage components because there exist too many loopholes for control to be effective. Quality and quantities are adjusted in the products, sales credits are shortened and terms are made less favourable for buyers, dividends are merely deferred for future distribution, and so on. Concretely, no incomes and prices policy has ever worked—not even during a war economy. Price controls inevitably lead to black markets or unofficial rationing on the distribution side and to some form of wage drift at the work level owing to the impossibility of applying national standards to the wide diversity of circumstances and exigencies prevalent in different industries and enterprises.

Virtually all the attempts to introduce some form of prices and incomes policy—ranging from formal price-wage controls in Holland, through the various mandatory/voluntary mixes, to the exhortatory guidelines of the late sixties in the United States—resulted in outstanding failures. There is good *prima facie* evidence to support the criticism that these policies not only did not work, but that they contributed to making the situation worse and were responsible for some of the current hyper-inflation in the UK, USA, Denmark, and elsewhere.

Despite such hard experience, advocates of the incomes policy are returning to the attack. Though hesitant to adopt formal and open positions because of the political risks involved, several governments are attempting to reintroduce controls, clandestinely or indirectly, notably in the USA, France, UK, Germany and Ireland. One of the clandestine approaches is the encouragement of private business to reject union demands over a certain level, backed by government refusal to conciliate disputes.

Private enterprise is encouraged by the mounting support drummed up by the economic and financial traditionalists: the Bank of England, the US Federal Reserve Board, and a majority of governors of central banks.

More and more leading bankers, industrialists and academics, having exhausted their knowledge and imagination on the intractable problem of inflation, rather than avow their helplessness are re-advocating the old incomes policy chestnut. Almost without exception, this group holds exaggerated wage rises to be the principal factor behind price inflation.

EXPERT OPINION

Professor Harry Johnson
Economist, London School of Economics
Sunday Times, March 1971

'I don't view the problem of inflation in this country as cost-push. Essentially I view it as the natural reaction of labour in the country to the effort to cut the real standard of living by devaluation. Devaluation was necessary but you can't expect workers simply to lie down under it. I think Labour delayed acting because of political pressure, and the change of government has allowed them to act with more speed than people expected, but I don't regard this as a major problem which requires a tremendous set of policy changes. The main danger, in fact, is that the Government will be stampeded by the country's economists and financial journalists into imposing an incomes policy which I don't regard as necessary. Apart from that, the Government may lack the determination to apply enough sustained pressure to keep the rise of wages within bounds. In other words, I think there's a danger of overshooting which could lead us into another balance of payments problem.'

Slightly to the left of these dollar-dinosaurs or money mastodons, as they have been called, stand those who would link both excessive wages and excessive profits together as the underlying causes of inflation. Professor John K. Galbraith (who conveniently for his theory is neither a worker nor a manager) claims that the power of corporations and trade unions today permits them to impose wage and price increases, through direct or indirect collusion, upon a powerless public, despite the introduction of mini-controls like credit restrictions and monetary and fiscal measures. He therefore advocates a total and permanent control of earned incomes and prices. The problem of reconciling full employment with price stability, he argues, will not be solved through management of aggregate demand, but through direct regulation. 'Eventually, we will have a permanent system of wage and price controls, for there is no alternative.' One is reminded of Professor Galbraith's equally affirmative prediction, made less than a year ago following the fall on the New York stock exchange, that by this time we would be in a deeper, uglier depression than in 1929. Both prophecies are most likely best forgotten.

A notable feat of adapting long-term prices and incomes policies to the hostile terrain of short-term economic conditions was achieved by the OECD under the stimulus of its Secretary General, Emile van Lennep, who seems to share the no-nonsense attitudes of those for whom inflation is exclusively and forever due to money wages rising faster than labour productivity. In perhaps the gloomiest report produced to date, the OECD (reflecting its political, nation-state constitution) opted for a large-bore shotgun approach to anti-inflation policy.

CURES FOR THE NEXT WORLD

Rejecting predominants or primary causes in a historic departure from all past practices, and seemingly from rational theory and common sense, the OECD declared that there were no panaceas, and advocated a policy mix of more than twenty factors. These ranged from demand management through income policies, active manpower programmes, psychological conditioning, anti-monopoly and foreign trade measures, and strengthening employers' resistance to criticism of 'over-aggressive use of market power by certain unions'.

A prescription of higher unemployment provoked such a hostile reception from some of the political pragmatists that it was abashedly cut out of the report, though it continues to be secretly applauded in the corridors as being courageous, hard-nosed and correct. But the new twist given to prices and incomes policy, of which the OECD has been a staunch advocate, is that 'despite the difficulties, the search for an effective price-incomes policy should not be abandoned; but this should be regarded as a long-haul operation . . .'. Even though, to quote Keynes, 'In the long run we are all dead'.

'Demand management' is an extremely dubious, updated technique designed to encompass both fiscal and monetary policy and to maintain a balance between the overall demand level of money incomes and the productive supply of goods and services. But the OECD blithely recommended its continued application.

On the one hand it stated that 'the control of aggregate

demand through fiscal and monetary policies has proved more difficult than foreseen by many economists a decade or so ago'. On the other hand it recommended 'that cautious demand management policies are required', which is a tried and tested formula for 'objectivists' to avoid committing themselves. Hence the plea for one-handed economists.

The analyses and recommendations of the OECD illustrate the disarray and impotence of traditional anti-inflation policies. By its qualifications of the usefulness of demand management in combating inflation, and by its downgrading of prices and incomes policy to a 'long-haul operation unlikely to yield miracles', the OECD, unwittingly perhaps, helped to illuminate the end of an epoch in both economic theory and policy.

Though still basing its outlook upon the theory that too much income and effective demand are pushing against too few goods and services, and still advocating a modified form of a permanent prices and incomes policy (probably more in the interest of justifying its own past inaccuracies than commending it to the future), the 1970 report of the OECD effectively relegated Keynesian and monetary theory to a very low status compared to the lofty heights of yesteryear.

IN MEMORIAM TO KEYNES, FRIEDMAN, ET AL.

The inflation conundrum has proved lethal to the theoretical high-fliers of the past decade. The reanimation of Keynesian economics, undertaken by the 'new economics' group of fine tuners in the United States (some of whom have used their Keynesian fame to go public on the New York stock exchange), has faded, and the meteoric but short-lived Friedman monetarism has passed its peak, heading towards oblivion. For the first time since the end of World War I, eminent, non-radical economists at the American Economic Association's 83rd annual meeting in Detroit late in 1970 dared openly to pronounce the death of the age of Keynes and to predict the demise of the monetarist counter-revolution. It was pointed out that the failure of traditional economic strategy to reduce inflation by damping down aggregate demand through judicious fiscal and monetary measures (both the Keynesians and monetarists accept their joint application in practice) was clearly proven in the fiascos of the incomes policies during the period 1965 to 1969.

Attempts by both schools to explain away their failings, and so salvage what little remains of their prestige (notably by asserting that what is wrong is not their economics but the government's politics), are not very convincing. Even the middle-of-the-road econometric school of Paul Samuelson (who dismisses the monetarists with the same ardour as he deprecates 'neanderthal Keynesianism') still remains convinced that modern economic management is feasible through judicious central anti-cyclical measures.

However, although the scepticism towards the theoretical framework of anti-inflation policy is deepening, there still remains the deep-seated conviction that the source of the problem is located in the cost-push of wage inflation.

Since ready economic substantiation of this conviction is not to hand, some attribute the pathology to non-economic factors such as rising workers' expectations, sociological transformations in the power structure, breakdown of common identification and feeling of solidarity in the community, and so on. Such motivational or behavioural drives are proclaimed the reasons for workers' irrational reactions to rational and scientific economic policies. The core of the problem, therefore, for these non-theorists, like their predecessors, is still to identify the causes of *wage*-inflation and apply new techniques and methods for bringing workers' incomes under control. They allege that it is the medication which needs refining, not the basic diagnosis of the ailment. The end result of all the discussion around this point remains a neurotic concern with adjusting the variables of the inflation equation, rather than re-examining and replacing the old parameters which are still accepted largely as given.

The assumption that wages lead to, rather than respond to, price increases is currently a widely accepted dogma outside trade union circles. It is this blockage which impedes theory and policy from moving out of traditional orbits into a new dynamic path for the future. But each phase of capitalist economic development has its chronic problem.

Before World War I, the problem was growth and creating employment. During the inter-war period, it was curbing the business cycle to prevent unemployment. Since the end of World War II, concern has been exercised to apply the 'spin-offs' of the technological revolution to industry. The next decade's problem is most probably going to be adjusting to unprecedented rates of economic growth. An acceleration in the velocity of economic change will place tremendous stress upon certain existing institutions, probably beyond their ability to assimilate without breaking up. Old relationships will no longer be valid, such as those which linked wages to profits and prices. Rampant inflation appears to be the most immediate consequence of the structural upheavals occurring in industry.

But qualitative structural change is what economics is all about today. The preoccupation of theorists with equilibrium, with achieving a static balance in prices, largely ignores the impact of structural change on wages, profits and capital. It is no longer feasible to deal with prices as a static element in a totally innovative, changing system.

INFLATION IN ECONOMIC THEORY

Neither is it feasible to approach inflation as a relatively homogeneous and easily-defined phenomenon, identical in all periods and in different economic environments. Even the dictionaries fail to provide unambiguous, uniform definitions. Throughout economic history the unsolved riddle and seemingly irrational causes of price rises have preoccupied and largely baffled the greatest minds of the dismal science. Inflation has remained an indeterminate, unresolved chapter in economic history.

Adam Smith's revolution in economic thought in 1776 redefined economic power in *The Wealth of Nations* as 'the ability to produce real goods and services rather than the hoarding and possession of gold', as had been proclaimed by the mercantilists. He explicitly rejected the proposition that wages were the cause of inflation and charged that the collusion by capitalists to fix monopoly prices resulted in prices and profits set at levels higher than wage costs, and the free play of market forces being justified: 'People of the same trade seldom meet together, even for merriment and diversion, but the conversation ends in a conspiracy against the public or in some contrivance to raise prices.'

The succeeding writings in the 1800s by both David Ricardo and Karl Marx oriented economic thinking to prices, wages and profits in the distribution of wealth. Their analysis of the role of prices in the unfair distribution of incomes, and inequitable sharing of wealth between owners of capital and receivers of earned incomes has remained the cornerstone of progressive economic philosophy down to our time. Adam Smith and David Ricardo, as well as Karl Marx, focused attention upon the politico-economic power structures' decisive influence on price formation.

The emergence and durable pre-eminence of the marginal utility theories, in the late 1800s and early 1900s, was in part the establishment's attempt to lift prices and inflation theory out of a power-structure matrix and place it within a mechanistic, technological system which filtered out moral or political value judgements. Under its dominance, economics turned from the power relationships of macro-economic analysis, to a concern with the aggregates of microscopic entrepreneurial behaviour, subject not to the power of monopoly groups, but to the mechanistic marginalism of the market place. Thus it effectively buried or walled-over the value judgements and criticisms of the classical social philosophers, and proclaimed by charts and tangent curves that patterns of power and monopoly could not produce inflation. Though some of the tenets on price formation of the marginalist counter-revolution undoubtedly were and are still valid today, the perfect competition microscopic basis of its system, which underlies much of the modern wage-push and demand-pull inflation theories, is not.

The marginalist counter-revolution reigned supreme over economic orthodoxy until the appearance of Edward H. Chamberlain's and Joan Robinson's theories of imperfect competition in the thirties and early forties. Since these theories emerged, oligopoly or imperfect competition among a few large sellers has been accepted by the keepers of the economic faith as a significant and substantial qualification of the free play of market forces and mechanistic marginalism, thereby restoring (at least in part) the power matrix of the price mechanism. Lately, support for the power theory of price setting has been strengthened by a growing literature, backed by impressive, empirical and statistical data, on the growth and impact of true monopoly conditions in numerous sectors of the economy. Many modern economists, thereby, insist that important branches of modern, science-based industry which require enormous amounts of capital, available only to already-established giants, create conditions closer to full monopoly than to imperfect competition. Though it may be argued that such monopoly conditions are still far from characteristic of the economy as a whole, growing segments of industry are increasingly being brought under such monopoly conditions and transferred out of the competitive 'market' sector.

The plague of the 'amplifying business cycle' and the near trauma of the Great Depression, especially in the developed Anglo-Saxon economies, brought forth the Keynesian revolution of the 1930s. The purpose of Keynes' General Theory was to seek controls for the problem of unemployment. Previous economic theories did not deal with unemployment, as both the classical or marginalist schools assumed that full employment was a natural condition of the market economy. From total concern with microscopic entrepreneurial decision-making, Keynes moved orthodox economic theory back to dealing with macroscopic national economy aggregates, a level it had vacated to Marxist-socialist thinking. It was through greater government spending, even in the face of budget deficits, that growth was to be stimulated and full employment achieved; and it was through reductions in government spending that inflation was to be checked. Thus fiscal policy (taxes and public investment) became the chosen instrument for achieving and maintaining equilibrium among the macro-economic aggregates of the economy, particularly consumption, investment and income.

Its quite notable success on the unemployment side was not matched, unfortunately, by a comparable success on the inflation side, which got progressively out of hand, and moved from moderate to high, hyper and run-away proportions. The criticism of Keynesian theory and policy is that its omissions in the area of the quantity of money and velocity of its circulation resulted in a critical disregard of the dangers of over-extending the money supply, and sacrificing prudent money and credit management to the central purpose of full employment and growth.

Led by Professor Milton Friedman and his Chicago followers, the monetarists initiated a counter-revolution against Keynesian theory in the middle sixties. Their opening attack was on the palpable failure of the Keynesian 'New Economics' to check a spiralling inflation in the US and the UK which spread around the world. Updating a Quantity Theory of Money going back at least to David Hume, the Scottish philosopher of the eighteenth century, the monetarists insisted that inflation was the root cause of economic disequilibrium and claimed it was due essentially to excesses in the creation of money and credit. Conversely, deflation, recession and depression, they claimed, were the results of inadequate rates of expansion of the money supply. In its most rudimentary expression, the money supply (currency and various forms of credit), which equals the national income, is the volume of money multiplied by its velocity of circulation. Achieving equilibrium, including stable prices and high levels of employment, according to this school, requires that the money supply be continuously adjusted to compensate for expanding or contracting tendencies in the economy.

Neither the Keynesians nor the monetarists differentiate between the activity of the public and the private sectors.

Consumption, investment, income and expenditures of both parts of the modern mixed economy are aggregated to give the totals for the economy as a whole. This facilitated the strong reliance of both theories on the public sector in analysing economic problems and prescribing remedial policies. This public-sector bias naturally favours simplification and concentration upon a single economic function as the primary operational variable: public investment through tax and fiscal policy for Keynesians; control of the volume of money through expansive or contractive monetary policy for the monetarists.

EXPERT OPINION

George Schultz
US Secretary of Economic Affairs

'Certainly you cannot make any case that what has happened to wage income is responsible for inflation . . . fiscal and monetary forces produced the inflation. . . .'

James Tobin
Economist, Yale University

'There's no question that excessive labour costs add to inflation. But if you want to put first things first, have a look at the role of profits.'

In respect to the current inflation, discussion has evolved through two distinct phases. During the period up to 1960 and into the early years of the past decade, the emphasis was on the 'demand pull' or monetary causes. Expanding public social expenditures, growing foreign trade, commitments to higher rates of growth through investment, accelerated private and public depreciation of capital equipment, etc. led to a strong rise in the rate of the money supply in most industrialized countries. From this came the seemingly obvious explanation that the price inflation was the consequence of too much effective demand chasing too few goods and services, or the demand-pull syndrome.

But suddenly it was observed that the behaviour of prices relative to demand no longer corresponded to the demand-pull pattern. Sales and incomes in several economic systems (US, UK, Italy, Denmark, Holland, Sweden, Norway, Turkey, Greece, for example) ceased rising; capacity operations in such key sectors as steel, autos, and household electrical appliances fell; net profits began to slide and other symptoms of a recession in the making appeared: *but prices kept rising*. Demand-pull or monetary inflation was obviously not the explanation, so the shift was made to the cost-push of wages emphasis. Cost-push, wage-based inflation, therefore, became the 'in' theory, and is the accepted 'immutable' explanation of the moment. Most of industry, the great majority of academics, and nearly all governments support this version of 'the' theory of inflation.

Throughout the evolution of economic thought, non-radical theory has reflected the community's concern with inflation and how to cope with the consequences of dynamic alterations in the amplitudes of price movements. Undoubtedly, all the theories from Adam Smith through to Ricardo, Marx, Marshall, Keynes and Friedman were formulated in response to differing specific problems and circumstances. While the symptoms of every inflation cycle appear to bear a close resemblance to each other, the causal factors varied widely during the different periods of economic history. An analogy can be made with the successive epidemics of flu. For the victims, one flu is like another: high fever, aches and pains, running noses, etc. However, for effective prevention, the vaccine must be specific to the virus constituting the epidemic, and there are a large number of these. A vaccine of Hong Kong flu viruses will not be effective for other Asian flu strains. Similarly, while the symptoms of the successive cycles of inflation may appear identical, the more potent causes triggering the process are probably quite distinct from one cycle to another.

All factors affect inflation—but some more than others

At the same time, past factors of inflation undoubtedly still influence prices, even if too much emphasis is placed upon them in succeeding phases. Policy-makers are therefore usually one cycle too late, as generals are usually one war in arrears. The process of inflation is certainly a wide-ranging, complex phenomenon. Ultimately, it is responsive to the multitude of individual decisions made constantly in both the public and private sectors of the economy. Most economic activities, therefore, eventually bear on price formation in an open economy. Besides actions by individuals and basic groups in the production and selling of goods and services, such factors as rising international trade, changes in regard to food and agriculture policies, the mounting social obligations for improved systems of education, social security programmes, collective infrastructure investment, and so on strongly influence price changes within a national economy. Government spending in these areas will likewise rise considerably in the seventies. To a very large extent, the practical consequences of a gathering insistence that the political economy concerns itself with the 'quality of life' and not with quantitative growth alone, will fall upon the government and lead to demands for augmented government expenditure. Improving the environment, ameliorating the social and political systems under intensifying pressure from irate and dissatisfied, even alienated, citizens—this will demand high technological capital investment.

EXPERT OPINION

Professor Robert Triffin
(*Noted authority on monetary problems*)

'For over twenty years one simple observation has guided my study of the monetary system. . . .'

'This relates to the origin and role of the periodic crises which, in this field as others, shake our institutions. These crises normally spring from our delay in adapting the institutions to new conditions and new needs. They are also an indispensable spur to the necessary reforms which governments, bureaucracies and public opinion will not otherwise accept.

'These crises serve the same purpose in the body social as illness does in the human one. A man does not worry about his liver until it hurts him. In the same way, we have not begun to understand, and correct, the malfunctioning of our successive monetary systems—from the gold standard to the gold-exchange standard and now the paper-exchange standard—until they hurt us.'

Unless education, both as to its content and orientation as well as to its physical plant and teaching personnel, is drastically overhauled, a wave of consuming anger will threaten most urban concentrations. Gerontology is a new science for an ancient shame—the suffering of elder citizens in an environment immorally laggard in concern for their needs. Forcing society to honour its responsibility towards the retired will be a major claim on scarce funds. Claims for organized leisure time will become the modern nightmare for public authorities generally. Trends towards the four-day week and three-day week are already discernable. More leisure time will first increase the cost of life due to the addition of eight hours of leisure activities entailing greater expenditure. An extra movie, week-end trips, eating out once more a week, will need more money. This will be paralleled by falling tax receipts as large numbers of people acquire sophistication in evading taxes, previously only the prerogative of those with very high incomes and capital gains to protect.

In addition to such general and continuing elements in the changing inflation picture, price movements and policy are also subject to pressures and circumstances peculiar to individual countries or groups of countries. The Vietnam war has been an important cause of inflation in the United States. According to the Pentagon, its direct costs already exceed $114 billion.[1] Chronic concern over its balance-of-payments

[1] Throughout this book, the term 'billion' is used to denote 'a thousand million' (i.e. American usage).

deficits, and exports and sterling balances, has been a major factor in the UK's approach to controlling inflation. Underdevelopment and underinvestment has conditioned such countries as Brazil, Argentina, Indonesia and the Philippines, to cite only a few, to living with galloping inflation, frequently exceeding 25% annually. And, of course, party politics and electoral strategies in the most democratic countries subjugate the economics of inflation to the imperatives of winning elections and catering to voters' self-interest at election time, as in the case of President Nixon's preparation for 1972; or to repaying financial backers upon winning power, as in the case of Tory Party policies in Great Britain.

Nevertheless, even allowing for the wide range of general and particular factors, a new and important inflation determinant has entered the contemporary picture. This is the rate and scope of structural changes taking place in the economies of the world, owing to the intensifying technological revolution and the globalization of markets and enterprises. Regardless of how rigorously and comprehensively inflation controls of the old order are applied, the objectives of price policies will not be attained unless these new parameters are recognized and suitable theories and approaches adopted. The relevance of policy based upon assumptions of demand-pull monetary inflation, or cost-push wage-cost inflation, has been decisively weakened. In the decade ahead, structural change, the multinational company, and capital investment will be the new determinants of inflation. They will not entirely supplant the others, but will reduce their relative significance in the inflation equation. As the experience of the last decade conclusively demonstrates, it is to this new dynamic partial sector that more attention and policy must be directed, rather than concentrate exclusively upon the functions which have proven not to generate the antibodies to fight these new strains of the inflation virus.

II. It is not Just Words—Things Really are Changing

Concurrently with the 'revolution in rising expectations' and transcending socio-political values, a tidal wave of structural change in industry has been building up. Its thrust has already transformed vital segments of the industrial environment and initiated a self-sustaining reaction within the economy's ecological chain. The mechanism of price formation has been intrinsically modified, though the phenomenon and its implications seem not yet to have penetrated official doctrine.

Economists and policy-makers have had a terrible time trying to predict trends. For one thing they have consistently underestimated the rate of growth, both nominal and real, which has been higher than official expectation. Recessions have not resulted from deflationary measures, high interest rates and scarce credit lines. New terms such as 'mini-depression', 'growth-recession', or 'stag-flation' were coined to label situations in which the economic factors related and combined in entirely new ways. Industrial investment did not recede substantially at any phase of the business cycle, and prices themselves did not move along traditional pathways. Contrary to common belief, prices of manufactured goods did not rise significantly in the period from 1958 to 1968. According to the OECD, the prices of manufactured goods in the seventeen most important industrialized countries rose on average in the range of 1% to 2·5% a year. This means that in the segment of the economy which employs the majority of workers, and pays out the largest share of wages and salaries, there was little inflationary pressure during a considerable part of the crisis period. In contrast, prices in the service and construction sector have risen considerably: 'together, these accounted for from 70% to nearly 90% of total price rise in the major countries over 1958–68', according to the OECD. In France, for example, during the period 1962–70, the index for services rose 79%, or just under 10%

a year. Manufactured products, by contrast, rose only 26%, or just over 3% a year.

The growing importance of the service industries represents a major structural change in the economy. It is a sector in which productivity rises least rapidly because it is difficult to automate and in which more capital investment and labour force (soldiers, teachers, barbers, knowledge processors) will be employed in turning out non-durable, subjective services, few of which will figure in cost-of-living indices. This sector is also the most difficult for unions to organize.

DISJUNCTION BETWEEN CAPITAL AND LABOUR-INTENSIVE INDUSTRIES

Under the impulse of science and technology a chasm is opening up between modern growth industries and the more traditional ones. The expansion of electronics, petroleum, chemical-process industries, plastics, pharmaceuticals and certain segments of the metal industry contrasts with the relative stagnation of agriculture, urban transportation, textiles, clothing, furniture, mining, construction, and similar industries. Applied automation has reached tremendous proportions in the process industries. The search for economies of scale, the application of centralized management and capital to more extensive markets, the thrust to conglomeration and multi-industry, multi-product enterprises is creating an inherently different type of industry to what exists in the traditional branches. The resulting contrasts and differentiation between them makes the analyses and policies of macroscopic economics less and less relevant to real behaviour, for the 'averages' of statistical data and assumptions based on 'average' or 'typical' industries have become increasingly unrepresentative of a major part of industry.

This is notably the case in respect of the effect of competition on the pricing policies of enterprises. To a very large extent, superconcentration has reached a point of no return. The notion of true competition has long been discarded, but today even the relevance of oligopoly theory, of market domination by a few giants operating under conditions of imperfect competition, is being queried. Between the few rivals who dominate most markets (four or five leading firms usually account for 50% to 80% of shipments of major products) prices are administered in a collective fashion.

EXPERT OPINION

OECD Observer

'The most interesting feature of 1969 and 1970—and also, perhaps the most disquieting—is that there has been noticably more synchronization in price movements than in demand conditions.'

Competition in modern industry is through channels other than prices: advertising, quality, discounts, product differentiation, integration of production and distribution, etc.

Productivity differences by branches are growing rapidly. In oil, chemicals and plastics, growth is three to four times faster than in printing, food and drink, leather, or mechanical equipment. A report issued by the European Economic Commission of the UN on productivity in Western Europe in 1970 stated:

'Productivity gains by branch vary quite widely, even if exceptional values (which may be due to faulty estimates or may represent only very minor branches in the country concerned) are ignored. The "typical" rate of increase for overall manufacturing productivity is taken to be 4·4%, and the "central range" is between 5% and 8% a year. The fastest typical rates, of 6% to 8% a year, appear in chemicals, oil and "miscellaneous" manufactures (which includes plastic products). Wood products and furniture also rank high. At the other extreme, typical growth rates are low—2½% to 3½% a year—in food, drink, printing, and in non-electrical machinery. But exceptions can be found to these rank orders in every branch.'

In fact these averages significantly understate the differentials relative to the rate of productivity growth within the top half-a-dozen or dozen firms which contribute to over 75% of the branches' output. Further, the range of the figures is less wide than it would be if they included the highest productivity countries in the top-ranked branches such as US, Japan, Australia, Latin America.

The report also confirmed that, on the issue of technology and productivity:

'The question posed is the extent of association between productivity gains and growth of total output. There is a great deal of evidence for this association, both on the aggregate level, when GDP or total manufacturing output are compared between countries, and on the branch level when the development over time of branches of industry in a single country are compared. The basic hypothesis is that fast productivity increases largely come from the opportunities of exploiting the opportunities for technical progress and economies of scale inherent in fast growth of output.'

NEITHER COMPETITION NOR MONOPOLY AFFECT PRICES VERY MUCH

Many economists, and those still clutching to the anti-trust philosophy, persist in believing there is a direct link between concentration and inflation. This opinion asserts, with little self-doubt, that high rates of concentration and high rates of profits unimpeded by competititive restraints inject an inflationary bias into the economy. It is contended that the line of constructive action is through anti-trust legislation and more competition.

Another and certainly more pertinent line of argument is that it is not size or oligopoly *per se* which causes inflation, particularly in regard to highly industrialized economies. As numerous studies confirm, bigness today means productivity and efficiency, regardless of the conventional antagonism towards concentration and the numerous cases to the contrary

TABLE II. 1. *Rates of increase in manufacturing output and labour productivity in Western Europe*

(*per cent per year* [*least square trends*])

Rank order of output growth	*Typical value*				*Central range*	
	Output per cent	*Output rank*	*Productivity per cent*	*Productivity rank*	*Output per cent*	*Productivity per cent*
Oil	12·7	1	7·5	1	8·7–16·4	6·2–9·0
Chemicals	10·5	2·5	6·3	2	8·7–14·0	5·5–7·9
Miscellaneous	10·5	2·5	5·8	3	8·7–13·0	4·9–6·8
Electrical machinery	9·1	4	4·5	9	6·3–12·8	2·7–6·0
Paper	8·2	5	4·4	10	5·9–9·6	3·4–5·1
Basic metals	8·1	6	4·7	7	4·9–9·6	3·4–5·4
Transport equipment	7·8	7	3·7	14	5·1–10·9	2·0–6·0
Non-electrical mach.	7·5	8	3·5	16	6·3–8·2	1·8–4·9
Non-metal minerals	7·4	9	4·6	8	5·6–8·6	3·6–5·9
Rubber	6·9	10·5	3·6	15	4·7–12·0	2·0–5·5
Metal products	6·9	10·5	3·8	12·5	5·9–8·4	3·2–4·9
Furniture	6·4	12	5·6	4	4·4–8·1	3·7–6·7
Drink	6·0	13	2·6	19	4·4–8·1	1·9–3·1
Printing	5·7	14	2·5	20	4·4–9·2	1·9–3·1
Food	5·1	15	3·0	17	3·6–7·2	2·1–4·2
Clothing	5·0	16	4·0	11	3·9–7·2	3·4–4·7
Wood	4·7	17	5·5	5	4·0–5·3	4·5–6·7
Textiles	4·5	18	4·8	6	2·8–6·4	3·9–5·3
Tobacco	3·0	19	3·8	12·5	1·2–5·0	1·7–6·4
Leather	2·3	20	2·8	18	0·6–5·2	1·3–4·0
Total manufacturing	6·6		4·4		5·0–18·0	3·7–5·5

Source: *Economic Survey of Europe in 1970*, ECE/UN, April 1971.

which can be cited. In most capital-intensive industries in the US, UK, Germany, or Sweden, for example, the four or five firms which ship from 40% to 80% of a given product have higher value added and shipments per employee figures than the smaller, more labour-intensive firms.

A study on *Concentration and Productivity* in the US, published in 1969 by the authoritative National Industrial Conference Board, based upon examination of the largest firms in 348 industries in 1963, confirmed that size, high productivity and low labour costs correlate directly in modern industry. It found that the first four companies in the top quarter of the industries compared with the remaining companies in the industry 'were at least 50% more productive than other companies in the same industry regardless of the measures used, . . . in half of the industries the top four companies were at least 25% more productive and in three-quarters of the industries the top companies were at least 9% more productive. . . .' In an analysis of 35 leading productivity industries, including food and kindred products (14 industries), chemical petroleum and allied products (12 industries), and 35 bottom-productivity industries, including apparel (15 industries), leather products, textiles and lumber and wood products, the study found that average (median) value added per employee in the highest productivity group was approximately four times the average value added for the bottom group—with the top set averaging $23,000 and the bottom set averaging $6000 per employee. The value of shipments accounted for was only 9% in the top group compared to 34% for the bottom group.

The report concluded:

'Although these findings are hung on bare statistical skeletons, the consistency of their alignment points toward a pervasive relationship between company size and productivity on the one hand, and between productivity and concentration on the other.

'These relations suggest that where the indicated correspondence between productivity and concentration holds an individual industry, raw data on concentration or company size are not necessarily reliable indicators of anti-competitive behaviour. And this, in turn, suggests that if anti-trust policy were to rely heavily on such raw data, the resulting enforcement programme would run the risk of lowering productivity rates below those that would be reached if criteria were aligned with a wider array of relevant industry and company facts.'

As a result, the large firms could more easily lower prices than the less efficient, smaller firms. If they are not doing so, it is because of price-setting agreements between themselves and with the smaller ones, whose marginal costs are much higher. A corollary of this line of reasoning is that with more monopoly and less firms in an industry, prices would tend to be lower rather than higher. But, of course, this is a pipe dream. The bigger they are, the larger they grow and the higher the prices they set to increase their retained earnings. As in the case of competition's marginal influence on prices, it is not the needs of the inefficient firms which determine their price policy but their unlimited capacity for absorbing capital. Lower prices would not result either from measures to increase competition nor to strengthen monopoly. The era when prices reflected the marginal utility of goods for consumers, if they ever did, is definitely over. Today, prices of consumer goods which have reached market maturity and are mass-produced travel at slower or faster rates in one direction only—upwards.

Between 1000 and 2000 enterprises today account for over 75% of the Western world's industrial output. Less than 200 of the 200,000 American firms possess between them over 60% of the country's capital. Fifty leading UK firms account for 75% of the country's exports. Six Japanese industrial giants produce nearly half of the nation's GNP; and around 150 Canadian companies account for between 60% and 70% of all business investment.

A report prepared by the Senate Subcommittee on Anti-Trust and Monopoly, almost a decade ago, calculated the share of output controlled by the four largest companies in each of several hundred industries. Just a few familiar products, drawn from this list, illustrate the extent of concentrated control over American industry. The four largest companies in each of their respective industries produce the following proportions of the nation's output of these products:

100% of railroad passenger cars
99% of primary aluminium
98% of plate glass and flat glass
98% of automobiles
96% of photographic film
95% of outboard motors
94% of copper products
93% of electric light bulbs
83% of salt
82% of cigarettes
81% of tin cans
80% of towels and washcloths

The most recent official survey on industrial concentration in France, published in January 1970, shows that 20% of French companies account for 90% of total business. Nearly 64% of the smallest of the 200,000 firms examined accounted for only 5·3% of the national turnover. At the top, 0·4%, or 800 firms, which do annual business of over $20 million, account for 37% of the total output. Holland's top six firms completely dominate the economy and foreign trade; as do FIAT, Montedison, Olivetti and IRI in Italy; and Société Générale, Solvay, Petrofina and a few others in Belgium.

Joint ventures and financial links are extensive and growing between the giants, and this further reduces the possibility of meaningful price competition. Certain writers are convinced that by 1985 some 200 to 300 corporations will control 80% of the West's productive assets. The enormous sums of capital required to enter this élite group assures shelter and protected positions for those few firms able to raise the necessary amounts. It effectively excludes small- and medium-scale firms from an increasingly important segment of the economy which employs the most capital and produces the most goods.

A SINGLE POLICY DOES NOT WORK

The consequence of such concentration is that the chasm between the modern capital-intensive sector (which is progressively getting more of the total investment funds) and the traditional sector is becoming more difficult for macro-economic policies to span. Public policies are confronted with the dilemma that measures designed to influence the overall economy are limited in their principal effects to the marginal, regressive, labour-intensive sector, instead of affecting the expanding sector. The real bite of policy depends in large measure on the composition of the economy in respect of the two sectors. As the relative importance of the capital-intensive sector grows, the power of public macro-economic policies becomes diluted. This has already reached a level sufficient to cause concern in highly industrialized countries, in regard to such matters as foreign trade, inflation and employment. In these areas, public policy has the strongest impact on the less important sectors and a lesser impact upon the key branches whose activities are most relevant.

EXPERT OPINION

George J. Sitaras
Department Head of Production Division Facilities, Otis Elevator Co., USA.

'Some analysts are surprised that Federal efforts to control inflation have not had a greater effect on corporate plans to acquire equipment.

'In general, manufacturing engineers preparing proposals for the acquisition of new production equipment are not directly influenced by Federal tax and monetary regulations. This is not to say that Federal regulations have no effect on acquisitions. Investment credits, depreciation guidelines, tax sur-charges, etc., may affect corporate decisions to increase or hold off on expenditures for capital equipment. They may also affect some marginal proposals for cost improvement or plant expansion. However, proposals least affected are those dealing with the acquisition of equipment for replacement of old, worn-out, or obsolete equipment or equipment essential to maintain profitable operations—and these are the most serious problems facing most manufacturers.

'Manufacturing engineers preparing proposals for new, advanced facilities must be guided by technological advancements and those projected trends that reflect natural economic growth—and not variable Federal regulations. . . .'

Government fiscal and monetary policy is obviously most efficacious in the public sector of mixed economies. But it influences behaviour in the private sector much less than is generally assumed. It is becoming more and more evident that pressing an incomes policy in the public sector does not give the hoped-for results in the private one, which has a different games plan and programme than that of the government. For example, regulating the money supply along traditional lines, on the assumption that prices, wages and investments are interdependent and rise during expansion and contract during recessions, is not working effectively. During contractions, conventional fiscal policy, assuming prices fall, calls for promoting a reduced level of overall spending. But in fact falling sales incline firms to raise prices to assure their liquidity; for smaller ones price rises are necessary sometimes to avoid bankruptcy. The large firms, given their credit status, can usually outbid the smaller ones for scarce investment capital. And in any case most of the national restrictions of the money supply are circumvented by the corporate use of the global sources such as Eurodollar borrowing, Eurobond issues, and transfer loans from subsidiaries situated in countries where the money market is not tight. Also for modern firms which have expanded at a fast clip a pause usually provides a breathing space in which to trim off marginal activities, discontinue slow-moving products, and transfer assets out of less profitable operations. This invariably requires augmented capital. Consequently, even in down-turns, the modern firm is constantly in need of important amounts of liquid capital to implement its global plans which extend beyond the primary task of producing and selling products: i.e. financing, R & D, pulling off mergers, buying up majority of minority participations in foreign firms, forming joint ventures, creating overseas distribution chains, etc. Many of these activities are, indeed, best achieved during down-turns, when the objects of takeovers or amalgamations are short of capital and find it difficult to sustain sales. These activities have become as much a part of modern business as production, with the result that, regardless of the general health of the economy, the craving for capital is continuous.

CASE CAMEO

USINOR—Producer of a third of France's steel

A prospectus for raising a new capital issue states that a new ambitious investment programme of USINOR for 1971 to 1975 has been undertaken, estimated at 4 billion francs.

'. . . on the assumption that each of the following five years are equal to that of 1970, this programme, despite its scope, could have been entirely realized through autofinancing. It is only out of prudence that a certain contribution of new capital from stockholders, and in the form of loans, has been envisaged.'

'Since 1968 for an increase in turnover of 80%, cash flow has been multiplied by six. . . . Thus the cash flow/turnover ratio moved from 6·9% to 18·2% in 1969, to reach 23·4% in 1970.

'The improvement in the results of the company permitted a greater and greater amortization.'

In 1970 cash flow totalled 1·22 billion francs ($244 million) compared to a net profit of 220 million ($44 million).

Another important difference between the two sectors is that wages relate to prices in different ways. In labour-intensive industries, the tendency is for real wages and prices to move together. When prices rise, wages tend to follow, because employment, costs, sales and profits all increase. Conversely, unemployment, falling sales and lower profits tend to dampen and reduce real wages in the down-turn. Government policy is synchronized with the labour-intensive industries, and its anti-cyclical measures are in phase with the movements of wages and prices in this sector. The reverse is true in the case of the capital-intensive industries. During the expansion, with total or near-total utilization of capacity, unit labour costs fall and nominal wage rises do not get incorporated into prices. In the contraction phase, even with stable money wages, unit labour costs rise due to reduced sales and larger unused capacity. These higher unit costs are carried over into prices, contrary to the expected tendency towards falling prices in the economy as a whole. Thus wages and prices move in counter-cyclical directions, and incomes policy, which is out of phase with the capital-intensive cycle, aggravates price rises in the upturn, rather than mitigates them. For example, making money scarcer and costlier during the expansion phase causes firms to raise prices to ensure adequate capital when unit wage costs tend to be lower. And in the contraction phase an expansive fiscal or tax policy does not compensate for higher unit labour costs and reduced sales, which also causes firms to put up prices in the monopoly segment of the market.

When larger firms need capital, they raise it, regardless of market liquidities or interest rates. Unit labour costs, the relation of wage rates to prices like investments and sales strategies, involve a different set of calculations to those prevalent in the less invested, less concentrated sectors. It is a grievous fact that a country's aggregated policy is ill-equipped to handle these problems of the structural gap.

Such policies have already begun to appear impotent, more productive of chaos and conflict than promotive of stable and orderly growth. Because of the proportions assumed by concentration and monopolization in the capital-intensive industries, a large and progressively expanding group of enterprises is effectively beyond the reach and control of public policy.

III. Technology on the Rampage

Rampaging technology will accelerate the obsolescence of both human skills and machinery. The formulation of manpower policies appropriate to new technology will require profound readjustments in the training of young workers and the retraining of adults on a continuing basis. New, active labour-market systems will be required to enhance geographical mobility and the transfer of skills to where jobs exist.

The new approaches to solving manpower problems will cost a great deal of money to develop, but they will cost industry a great deal more if they are not developed.

The past decade produced technological breakthroughs which changed the face of entire industries. One of these was the flat-glass process, costing Pilkington's over $500 million in R & D to bring on the global market, which transformed the entire flat-glass industry of both the West and the East. In the USA, the UK and German plants—as in Soviet, Polish and Czech plants—thirty-six men operate the entire process.

Another breakthrough was the extension of integrated computer control systems through a complete process to replace automatically-controlled, individual closed loops, thus making possible completely automatic computer controls in oil and certain branches of chemical refining (notably intermediates).

On the near horizon are an unprecedented number of new processes and products which promise to alter profoundly the structure of other industries as well. The world's first commercial synthetic wood-pulp plant may soon be built in Japan through a joint American–Japanese venture.

Crown-Zellerback have developed a 'pulp' which will be ethylene-based. It will be used to produce plastic-based paper. BASF is known to have run successful pilot plants in Germany for producing synthetic textiles on a continuous extrusion line, thereby eliminating the spinning and weaving stages of the process. Other companies have developed competing systems for 'casting' synthetic tissue into the future, and these are due shortly to come on the market.

DuPont de Nemours, the world's largest chemical firm, informed its stockholders that it has twenty-five entirely new and different products at varying stages of completion for marketing in the next decade. Around 50% of the whole chemical industry's products for 1980 are in the laboratory today.

EXPERT OPINION

H. J. Kahn
Fisons Ltd

'The chemical industry is perhaps the most typical of the science-based industries of high technological content which now account for half the output of the advanced Western industrial nations. These industries are characterized by their high rate of growth, their increasing share of world trade and the international marketing by manufacturers of their own products. Their roots are firmly embedded in the concept of devoting a consistently high proportion of income to innovation from research.'

Many other areas of technology hold the continuing attention of corporate planners. Plastics and synthetics—classic materials of what has been called the 'Second Industrial Revolution'—are bound to grow in significance. The whole realm of pharmaceuticals—antibiotics, sulfas, insecticides, psychothropic agents, and the like—will prosper in the remainder of the century.

The social technologies for organizing endeavour and distributing its results will undergo marked change. Man will enjoy continued enlargements in his ability to control the life of animate and inanimate things, alter the characteristics of materials, extend his sensory capacities, and mechanize physical and intellectual processes. As a result, the productive process and its environment will experience continued accelerating change.

In data processing, scientific research, handling payrolls, inventories and orders, as well as in setting gauges and adjusting valves in oil refineries, chemical plants and steel mills, computers became a pervasive feature of capital-intensive industry in the sixties. For the seventies, apart from their application to the knowledge industries, the major development promises to be computerization of machine operations. Until recently the diversity of manufacturing, both in machine operations and assembly, limited the application of the computer in the factory.

AUTOMATING MACHINE TOOLS

New versatile devices are now finding their way to the factory floor. Computer-directed machine tools, commanded by tapes, are taking over more of the machinery process. Already they control conveyors and warehousing systems. Some of the new machines on the planning board will be able to do assembly work. The machine tool industry, instead of supplying only tools, will shortly be required to provide entire production systems.

This development is only now commencing and therefore costs are very high at this stage. Even the new 'mini-computers' with modest capacities are still very costly. But there is little doubt that this economic bottleneck will be overcome in the course of the seventies and a new type of factory, heavy on equipment and very light on labour, will become the rule where today it is the exception.

The machine tool industry is unquestionably on the threshold of a far-reaching technological revolution, as the move towards 'total automation' acquires momentum. The marriage of the computer and the machine fuses job planning, material controls, inventory control, and machine maintenance into a co-ordinated flow process. This is definitely in the futurology of the modern factory, as it is already an existing feature of refineries and processing plants.

This trend towards a continuous type of production instead of batch-processing is invading a great many other industries. Steel, for example, in the new continuous flotation and extrusion processes, is moving closer to a complete flow process. In the rubber, paper, cement, or ceramic industries, similar computer-stimulated transformations are taking place which are turning the operations into process systems. All the changes are increasing the number of automated processes and speeding up the advance towards full-scale automatic production, entirely controlled through a central computer.

The magnitude of this revolution is already tremendous. For example, the United Nations estimates that over 80% of increases in gross national product is today contributed by technological progress and capital. In the United States and Sweden, where average wages and living standards are the highest in the world, the contribution of labour is estimated at only 10% of GNP—technology and capital account for 90% in the UN estimates.

When total automation invades the engineering industries this figure will become even greater.

A striking indication of the size of the problem involved in modernizing equipment is a recent study which reported the eye-opening finding that in the United States almost 20% of all industrial plants and equipment are more than twenty years old, and about 12% of the units in place are technologically obsolete.

CASE CAMEOS

American Iron and Steel Institute

The authoritative Iron and Steel Institute forecast investments in the US steel industry of more than $1·6 billion in 1971, a fall of 10% from 1970. The reason it states 'is the completion of numerous and important modernization programmes'.

Mr Eliji Toyota
President of Toyota Motors

Commenting in a press interview on his firm's 1970 results,

Mr Toyota stated, 'Net profits fell 10% in the half year ended November 30th, to 17·27 billion yen ($48 million), on sales which rose 14% to 441·54 billion yen ($1·23 billion).' The profit decline was attributed to a large increase in depreciation charges. The company noted that large amounts of new equipment were installed during calendar 1970, increasing production capacity to 2 million cars at a cost of almost $300 million. In an earlier press interview Mr Toyota said the firm plans to curb plant expansion, as capacity has increased fivefold in five years. Investments will not be curtailed but emphasis will be shifted to labour-saving and rationalization measures.

In manufacturing, the two most 'antiquated' industries technologically are the highest investment ones—petroleum and chemicals. The same study estimated that about $144·5 billion would be required for all business to replace its technologically obsolete equipment with 'the best new plants and equipment'. For less technically-evolved economies, the costs of replacing a comparatively much higher percentage of old or obsolete equipment becomes truly staggering.

WILL PRICES OR PROFITS PAY FOR R & D AND POLLUTION?

R & D expansion

Other new trends in industry are reducing the dynamic response of corporate capital investment to down-turns in the business cycle. Projections of long-term sales require larger current research and development spending. Total US private R & D expenditure in 1970 was a record $20·7 billion compared with $17 billion in 1968. It is expected to jump to $24·5 billion by 1973, a rise of 18% over 1970. British industry spends about $1·1 billion a year currently, with ICI and Unilever accounting for 10% of this. In France, R & D represented only 3% of GNP in 1960; by 1980 it will rise to 10%.

Twenty years ago, Japan bought twenty-five technical

licences for each one that it sold itself. Today, the ratio has been reduced to 10 to 1, and it will continue falling, for the period of the industry of imitators is drawing to a close. R & D expenditures rose to around $3 billion in 1970, and is projected at more than $6 billion in 1975. And, as in every other industrialized country, the expenditure is going heavily into chemicals, plastics, electronics, computers and space.

Similar rates of growth in R & D can be expected for most industrial countries. Large corporations will be compelled to expand R & D in order to retain their share of future sales and ensure their place in the innovation of products and materials.

From an activity which has been largely government-financed in relation to military needs (nearly two-thirds of all American R & D was federal Government supported in 1963, and slightly less than half in the UK, France and Sweden), than economically motivated, R & D is taking up more and more of industrial expenditures. Primarily it is being concentrated in the science-based, high technology industries. In fact the new modern capital-intensive sector is dependent upon such expenditure for its growth and prosperity. Increasingly, therefore, the ratio of such expenditure to capital investment will grow as the science-based sector becomes the dominant part of the world's economy.

The principal R & D sectors are the science-based industries of aircraft, electricity and chemicals, which take up from nearly half to three-quarters of the total investment in R & D in the principal industrial countries. Because they are capital-intensive they automatically become research-intensive. Aircraft R & D takes up over a quarter of such investment in the US, UK and France, which alone have built up airframe industries.

In electronics, where R & D is the key to expansion and growth, US research expenditures in 1968 were over $6·1 billion. Actually electronics research takes up nearly a quarter of total research expenditure in the US, 15% in the UK, and 12% in the Common Market. Between 70% and

TABLE III. 1. *The Structure of R & D expenditure in manufacturing industry*

(In percentage of total manufacturing industry)

		Science based				*Mechanical*				*Other*			*Total*
		Aircraft	*Elect.*	*Chem.*	*Total*	*Mach.*	*Basic Metals*	*O.T.E.*	*Total*	*Allied Prods*	*Misc. Prods*	*Total*	
United States	1963–64	38·3	24·8	13·0	76·1	8·0	2·6	8·9	19·5	2·5	1·9	4·4	100·0
France	1964	24·6	28·6	19·4	72·6	7·6	5·3	5·8	18·8	4·6	4·0	8·6	100·0
Canada	1963	16·9	29·1	23·6	69·6	4·2	9·8	0·9	14·9	5·4	10·1	15·5	100·0
United Kingdom	1964–65	29·0	24·5	14·4	67·9	8·4	8·7	7·3	21·4	6·7	4·0	10·7	100·0
Germany	1964	†	31·2	34·7	65·9	19·6	8·4	†	28·0	4·7	1·4	6·1	100·0
Belgium	1963	1·5	20·3	43·8	65·6	5·0	18·1	0·6	23·7	3·7	7·0	10·7	100·0
Japan	1964	*	30·3	27·3	57·6	5·1	9·4	11·3	25·8	8·4	8·2	16·6	100·0
Sweden	1964	19·8	24·3	9·9	54·0	13·9	13·1	7·8	34·8	4·1	7·1	11·2	100·0
Italy	1963	*	25·7	28·1	53·8	10·5	5·6	20·1	36·2	9·1	0·9	10·0	100·0
Austria	1963	*	18·6	24·0	47·6	4·0	24·9	16·3	45·2	4·0	3·1	7·1	100·0
Norway	1963	*	22·0	21·3	43·3	6·6	23·4	5·3	35·3	6·1	15·3	21·4	100·0

* Included in 'other transport equipment'.
† Included in machinery.

Source: OECD – *Report on R & D*

80% of this electronics research is now carried out in private industry.

The mechanical industries and basic metals, with one exception, account for under 35% of the total research expenditure, and miscellaneous and allied products vary between 5% and 21%. The science-based 'Big Three', therefore, already receive the bulk of the funds, and will receive an increasingly larger share in the future.

The table on p. 46 presented to the OECD ministerial meeting on science in 1968, provides a break-down of R & D between the different industries.

Pollution

The greater the threat of the pollution of man's environment grows, and the more accurately the thresholds are calculated in the 'permissible levels' of air, water and solid-waste contamination, the higher the costs to the consumer will be. Even to get the contamination cycles under control and in equilibrium in the US, according to the best estimates, will cost around $80 billion, almost as much as the entire fixed capital investment in that country for a year.

Automobile firms are calculating increases of 4% to 6% on the prices of new cars to cover costs incurred in adapting motors to required standards of hydro-carbon and carbon-monoxide emissions. Reducing or eliminating the sulphur oxides, nitrogen oxides and particulates from power plants and industrial operations; stopping the disposal of toxic effluent from chemical plants into adjacent lakes and rivers; stopping the disposal of mercury wastes by both the chemical and paper industries; removing dangerous chemical additives used in flavouring, colouring and preserving canned and packaged foods; suppressing phosphates and enzymes in detergents from the soap manufacturers; preventing spills and tanker collisions among the oil companies; removing thousands of ineffectual and several dangerous drugs from public sale by the drug companies; replacing DDT-based herbicides and pesticides with costlier but less harmful antibiotics—these are only some of the pollution problem areas which must be tackled. Eliminating them will be costly, especially to the consumer who will probably pay most of the costs in the end through higher prices.

EXPERT OPINION

Russel Train
Chairman President of US Council on Environmental Quality

'The cost to industry of abating pollution will generally be passed on to consumers just like the other costs of doing business . . .

'There will be complaints that business is shifting to the public a burden that it should carry. But it is the consumer who enjoys the product and should pay the cost of producing it.'

M. Robert Poujade

French Cabinet Minister for Environment
February 1971

'I recognize that the struggle against pollution is not without cost. It can now represent 5% to 10% of the costs of industrial enterprises. We must remember that we are in a world where international competition is severe.'

US News and World Report
January 1971

This US publication quoted a top adviser to President Nixon as saying, 'Environment is something that a lot of people are concerned about. . . . But sooner or later, consumers and taxpayers must realize that they are the ones who will pay for clearing up the environment and they will have to decide how much they are willing to pay.'

New systems of incentives and penalties are being sought for transferring some of the burden to those responsible and imposing heavy fines upon the firms and industries which are the worst offenders. But by and large it will be through taxes and prices that costs will be met. The government will need a great deal more income to finance anti-pollution programmes, and, as most industrial pollution derives from processes and products common to the entire industrial sector and not just to one firm or group of firms, higher environmental standards will automatically mean higher social costs. This expenditure, as in the case of incomes in the service trades, is not related to greater outputs of goods. As the intimate relationship between fatal coronaries and blood cholesterol build-up becomes known to growing millions of people, the switch away from polysaturated fatty foods will probably cause tremors, if not quakes, throughout agriculture and farming, especially dairy farming and much of animal husbandry.

These are pure cost factors, and, like securing the cessation of smoking, will probably be compensated through higher prices on other products. These changes in emphasis will represent enormous income losses. Some governments would lose up to 30% of their revenue if all their citizens gave up tobacco. Enterprises, if taxed to make up the short-falls in public revenues, will not accept lower profit levels, even if it means lower taxes; such moves would rather necessitate price rises to recover income for investment.

The staggering amounts of money involved make wage incomes and price forecasts hazardous. Unless, of course, our economic system decides that a certain margin of contamination and slow self-destruction is desirable for achieving balanced growth without inflation.

By the year 2000, seven out of every ten workers in modern industrial societies will be employed in the service industries and only three in production. The ratio was the inverse in 1960—seven in production and three in service trades. The ability of fully-automated processes to supply the spiralling demand of service incomes with material consumer goods will be crucial to achieving even a modicum of balance in the economy. Society's sanity and its relative peace and tranquillity will be more threatened by a shortage of automation than by atomic weapons.

All of these structural transformations and the crises which their shifts will precipitate may seem disparate and unrelated. However, they have one overriding common quality. They all will require fantastic amounts of capital expenditure to evolve solutions and help people adjust to the intrinsically different conditions of life engendered. The immediate capital needs are already half as much again as they were a decade ago. By 1980, capital spending will have to be double the 1970 rate if unprecedented crises are to be averted.

The need for capital in the seventies will escalate into the decade's special dilemma. It is already a problem of today's society in transition, and the principal cause of its new strain of global inflation. Liquidity will be the business problem of the decade. The crisis will arise from the capital goods sectors expanding exponentially and the consumer goods sectors arithmetically.

This growing imbalance cannot be adjusted by the modest measures available to governments. Whether consumer demand is dampened or wage-costs subside, the critical mass of capital accumulation will produce a run-away reaction unless the rate of capital growth is controlled.

The real cost of money, regardless of the amount in circulation or freshly emitted by the central banking systems, will rise swiftly under pressure of accelerating structural changes inherent in the system. This is the new element of the modern inflation, the virus against which no present vaccine is effective.

CAPITALIZING ON UNEMPLOYMENT

A crucial transformation in capital spending patterns has taken place during the last ten or twelve years which has remained undetected by the economic sentinels in their ivory towers and by the computers in their concrete skyscrapers.

No longer are increasing output and capacity getting the bulk of investment, as has been assumed, but rather this is being ploughed into automation and new technology to replace workers and reduce labour costs. Higher profit margins are sought more through modernization than through expanding output and sales. To the extent that sales are a consideration, it is sales in the future not the present which count. Already 65% of the West's total capital investment is for greater technological efficiency or labour displacement, and only 35% for augmenting capacity upon which employment and living standards ultimately depend.

The failure to account for this shift in capital spending from capacity to technology is probably a major reason for much of the irrelevance of economic theory under modern conditions.

The basic Keynesian equations assumed that total demand for capital and consumer goods affected spending and output in a direct linear fashion. Both industrial investment and higher wages in the prescribed functions complemented and mutually strengthened each other for better or for worse, depending on the phase of the cycle. Aggregate demand either rose or fell according to the parallel movement of investment and consumption.

The technological coefficient of industry was taken either as an independent variable or a secondary element in the interactions of the factors of production during the different phases of the business cycle. Fixed investment was held to be directly related to the short-term outlook of consumer demand, even though it led and lagged in the up-turns and down-turns.

The neo-classical and probably most pertinent economics in regard to the business cycle, national incomes and employment, holds that among the indogenous and exogenous factors affecting economic fluctuations, the most decisive is fluctuation in investments or capital goods.

EXPERT OPINION

Sir Frederick Catherwood
UK Director General of the National Economic Development Office
April 1971

Industrial investment in the UK could be far more buoyant 'given anything like reasonable cash flow and even the mildest confidence in the future'.

The rate of industrial investment is 'nowhere near its proper level', and he points out that a further drop is forecast for this year.

'All we can say is that, despite the tough squeezes of the last five years, despite extremely high interest rates, despite all the uncertainties of economic policy, the rate of industrial investment has not yet turned down as it did in the earlier and much milder credit squeezes of the fifties and early sixties.'

Sir Frederick stressed that without a higher investment rate with a much higher rate of replacement for obsolete plant, the UK is unlikely to hold its share of world trade, let alone regain any of the trade it has already lost.

He suggested that now it is generally accepted that if UK stocks of machine tools are twice as old as Germany's or Japan's, then the quality and cost of its engineering output is unlikely to be competitive.

'And it is now accepted that if the German motor industry or the Japanese steel industry invest at twice our rate, then our world market shares in cars and steel—including our share of our own market—are unlikely to improve and all the devaluation in the world will not make any difference to the disparity in industrial capacity.'

Investment in fixed capital, modern theory holds, is influenced by such factors as technological innovation, growth of population in terms of numbers, tastes and socially-conditioned needs, and the extension of markets and communications, etc. Investment, because it generates demand for both consumer and capital goods (through wages of workers in the former and demand for machines in the latter), is part of a self-generating process: the greater expectations of consumer demand lead to higher demand for capital goods which in turn raises total demand, and so on into a spiral. The cut-off of this self-generating force is supposed to occur when income growth, technological innovation and the real cost of capital become jointly unable to sustain the rate of net new investment.

The 'multiplier' or 'accelerator' effect requires that consumer demand has to keep increasing at a certain rate in order for a given level of investment to even remain stable. Therefore, the capital goods sector which displays the greatest cyclical movement is held to be functionally dependent upon changing expectations in consumer demand.

The fit of this theory to modern industry is very much looser than it was in the period in which it was first formulated. One of the principal causes for the change in emphasis has been the changing net effect of capital investment upon employment. Investment in technological innovation, because its purpose is to substitute automatic processes for labour, ultimately lowers employment. True, the investment in capital-intensive facilities has the immediate effect of creating jobs, and hence consumer demand, during the construction phase of the project. However, once the facility goes 'on stream', and begins its intended production programme, the longer-term effect is a net drop in employment due to the higher capital/labour ratio compared to the older, less capital-intensive operations it is replacing.

An interesting example of labour displacement through investment occurs in the case where government incentives to invest in under-employed development areas results in high capital-intensive technology competing away the employment in the less efficient more labour-intensive industries in the area. Instead of the investment generating employment opportunities, it ends up reducing them further still.

As the ratio of investment in technology to investment in capacity (T/Ca) becomes larger, this inverse effect becomes sharper. An increment of growth in capital investment produces a net decremental effect in employment. The psychological effect of rising unemployment accentuates the overall decremental effect further.

This decremental effect becomes greater as the T/Ca ratio of the investment function rises, for when the ratio is less than 1, each monetary unit of investment will progressively reduce demand and employment more than it will increase the volume of consumer goods and services.

These factors cannot be treated as two integral parts of the same total function any longer. The equation $D = C + I$ is not valid in the sense that a rise in either C (consumption) or I (investment) increases D (total demand). The new equation would have to be written as $D = C + (Ca/T)I$ which could produce a fall in D even when C and I are both rising if Ca/T is less than 1.

An analogous inversion of theory derives from direct foreign investment. When foreign investment is in funds being sent abroad and not in capital goods and equipment, which is usually the case, the neo-classical assumptions on the behaviour of investment are similarly modified. One of the effects is that investment does not create wages in the capital goods industries because the equipment is purchased outside the economy. Another effect is that it is not the changing outlook by corporations to consumer propensities and effective consumer demand at home which determines such investment, but conditions outside the local economy. This is an inflationary situation from a double standpoint. It takes capital funds out of the economy and encourages corporations to keep price levels high, even when consumer demand is falling at home, to maximize retained profits for transfer abroad. Secondly, the investment does not serve to augment the volume of goods and services and accordingly does not dampen consumer prices. The result is that the 'multiplier effect' is inoperative, because the self-generation of demand simply does not occur. Thus foreign direct investment, in its immediate impact, does not help reduce unemployment or turn the economy around during down-turns, whatever its other advantages and benefits may be to the economy and to society generally, which are admittedly very considerable.

Currently, net annual overseas capital spending from the US is around $12–$14 billion. Total US private capital spending for 1971 is forecast at around $82–$83 billion. The ratio of foreign to domestic expenditure will grow rapidly from 15% to 30% in a decade. When it reaches the $20 billion figure, the repercussions will be quite serious. Even with a very much higher rate of outside investment in the US, a net annual capital flight of such volume cannot fail to have powerful repercussions.

Therefore, the $D = C + I$ equation must again be modified to include another investment coefficient which does not automatically raise output, stimulate consumer demand, increase employment, or raise the volume of consumer goods in GNP. In fact if foreign plants export to the home market, the GNP can be decreased through such investment.

Thus it is perfectly conceivable with present trends that both the domestic and foreign components of investment could have negative effects on output, employment and overall demand. Although no dependable figures are available, 12% is not an exaggerated estimate of the proportion of foreign to total investment in the US. Added to the 65% for technological investment, this would raise non-capacity, non-employment investment to nearly three-quarters of the total.

That more capital funds in the world are being used to eliminate labour at home and substitute for it abroad than to expand the volume of goods and services, is a transformation of the highest importance. The almost total failure of economists and public policy-makers to have understood the implications of the structural change is a measure of the void which exists between industrial reality and the institutions supposed to have control over industrial activity.

Unless policies are changed to take account of this new dimension of investment-inducing technological change, no amount of public spending or fiscal and monetary measures will prevent inflation and unemployment rising together, for they are rigorously linked through the modern investment function.

THE TRADE-OFF THEORIES

If one were to take an x-ray photograph of unemployment around the world, it would reveal profound structural differences in its composition to that generally assumed in the macro-economic models. The diversifying and differentiating forces which technology is producing in industry have altered the types and causes of unemployment. It is no longer merely a question of a general down-turn or of cyclical movements in the economy caused by inflation, inappropriate levels of consumption and investment, imbalances in foreign trade, etc. Structural and technological unemployment is not caused by or eliminated by inflation or by anti-cyclical government policies, except very indirectly and in modest degrees.

For example, almost 50% of the nearly 6 million unemployed in the United States are victims of structural and technological changes, and 50% owe their conditions to general economic or cyclical causes. In France, experts estimate that 40% of the unemployment is of a structural nature, in Belgium over 60%, in Italy nearly 70%. Such technological and structural unemployment is largely unresponsive to public spending and fiscal policies, and although inflation does not cause it, increased capital spending intensifies it.

Industry-wide unemployment, as in the textile industry, or coal mines, will not be absorbed by new public and private spending. In France, acute shortages of workers exist in certain trades like the electronic specialities, optics, photography, precision mechanics, radio construction, household appliances, and telecommunications, along with relatively important overall levels of unemployment: between 500,000 and 700,000. Regional unemployment is another type which is immune to global investment plans, and is aggravated by specific, high-technology investments in an underdeveloped or receding industrial region. The north of France and Lorraine, the Ruhr valley in Germany, the Walloon and Limbourg regions in Belgium, Appalachia and Kentucky in the US, Quebec in Canada, southern Italy, western Ireland and Scotland will not have new jobs created through a general rise in national investment. On the contrary, the higher technology coefficient of the new investment will accentuate the difficulty even more, unless plans are specifically designed to meet the employment needs of these regions.

Early in 1971, Britain's unemployment rate topped 800,000, as a consequence of the government's continued 'anti-inflationary' policy. In the 1971–2 budget to March, the government introduced modest cuts both in personal income taxes and corporation taxes, designed to inject some buoyancy into the demand function and to absorb some of the slack. But the likelihood of these measures getting the unemployment figure down to around the 300,000 or 400,000 mark is slim, even if the reflation works. A large portion of the total is apt to reveal itself as fixed and not re-absorbable, given that the down-turn in many branches and large firms was utilized as an occasion to restructure and re-dimension longer-term operations in regard to the labour force, rather than as a classical reduction in employment due to immediate reduced levels of sales.

According to common standards, the nearly 6% of US unemployment is not high, and should be readily absorbed in any reflation of the economy. But this is not likely to take place, for a large part of this unemployment is special and specific. Among black citizens, largely unskilled, the overall rate is 8·5%, for whom, without upgraded skills, jobs will not be available. White-collar unemployment jumped from 930,000 in 1969 to nearly 1,600,000 in 1971. A part of the problem is the automation of process systems being introduced in offices, which intensifies the specialization of job functions and makes it easier to reduce staff when business slows down.

Seasoned executives, high-income technicians and engineers alike are feeling the pinch. The US Department of Labour reports that unemployment among 'professional and managerial' workers rose to 410,000 in 1971. The crisis of the defence industries has reached dramatic proportions. With the cut-back in defence spending, missile and aircraft manufacturers have laid off hundreds of thousands of highly-skilled technical personnel. The giant Boeing aircraft company laid off over 50,000 employees, or more than half its work force. The ill-fated Lockheed workers are seeing their company close down upon them, a counterpart to the eight thousand Rolls Royce workers in the UK: all are victims of the ill-starred Tri-Star jumbo jet venture. Already reduced in numbers from 102,000 in 1968 to 43,000 in 1971, 7000 more Lockheed workers lost their jobs in Seattle because of the decision of Congress on the SST. The aerospace and defence firms are finding it very difficult to switch out of space and war into earth and civilian production. And even if they did find a route from military hardware and missiles to housing, mass transit, pollution and other critically-needed production to alleviate urban woes, the skill mixes and job experience needed would probably be so different that most personnel would remain unemployable without re-training and re-education. Aeronautical engineering and aircraft body building are technological orbits far removed from pollution and urban engineering. An estimated 50,000 to 65,000 of the nation's 1·5 million scientists and engineers are unemployed, according to the US Department of Labor. Many of these previously much-sought-after professionals face a unique problem: their carefully-cultivated skills have become unsaleable commodities in a tight job market.

Another inflation-less type of employment is the broad-scale use of foreign or migrant workers in Western Europe: over 3 million in France, nearly 2 million in Germany, 800,000 in Switzerland, 1½ million in the UK, 200,000 in Belgium, 100,000 in Holland, and over 200,000 in Sweden. Because of cultural changes and advances in living standards, nationals have left certain trades and industries which are now totally dependent upon migrant workers from less industrialized, low-wage countries such as Portugal (300,000) Spain (750,000), southern Italy (1·1 million), Greece (300,000), Turkey (100,000), Yugoslavia (500,000), and Africa (2 million). The building and construction industry in Switzerland; the auto assembly lines and the melting and casting shops of Renault, Volkswagen, Mercedes, etc.; the mines of Belgium and Sweden; heavy engineering in Holland; the shipyards of Göteborg in Sweden; and the catering trades everywhere would be scarcely able to operate without foreign or guest workers. The same is as true for agricultural field-hands across Europe, as for the Mexican 'wet-backs' in the fruit and vegetable industries of southern California. The effects of this type of employment upon wages and prices are not relevant to the conventional thinking which still passes for informed opinion in official spheres. In only a very limited sense do such varying types of technological, structural and cultural employment and unemployment (each a direct consequence of the amount and kind of investment in technology) relate to classical problems of price and wage policies.

EXPERT OPINION

Enterprise (leading French management publication)
January 1971

An article in *Enterprise* comments upon the 'mystery' of French investments: 'From 1969 to 1970, industrialists evaluate their expansion at 30% in value and 23% in volume. For 1971 they expect an increase of 14% in value. In November, 26% of the industrialists estimated that, if demand increased, they couldn't meet it because of a lack of equipment, while in 1967 only 13% were in such a situation.'

Among the explanations given is: 'The expenditures made are translated into accrued production capacity only after delays which can be quite long. One doesn't create a steel mill for example, in several months.

'A part of the investments is utilized not to increase capacity of production but to economize labour which is more and more costly. In this sense it is confirmed that the rise in salaries impulses a greater effort to raise productivity.'

Stewart S. Carr
Chairman of US Bethlehem Steel

Speaking on the economic situation in the US, Mr Carr referred to the alarming persistence of inflation related to the tendency of contracting productive investments and their orientation. 'A rising portion of expenditure is allocated to improving the quality of the environment, which is socially desirable but unproductive economically, while the source of real growth of incomes are the investments in materials and productive equipment. . . .

'We are approaching the pitiful economic condition of Great Britain, characterized by excessive wage demands coupled with an inadequate investment policy.'

Writing off the trade-off

Amongst the most ephemeral of the policy concepts being propounded relative to wages and employment, is the inflation versus employment trade-off. Behind the rhetoric surrounding the discussion of this concept is a raging, if subtle, economic conflict. It involves judgements on the true relationship between prices and unemployment, and the implications for government policy. Those who support the premise of the wages-employment nexus are advocating a vigorous, short-run government juggling act which alternatively trades off employment against inflation in one period, and prices against employment in another.

The source of the trade-off theory is the 1958 study of A. W. Phillips, of the London School of Economics, who studied the relationship between wages and employment in the United Kingdom from 1861 to 1957, and transposed the correlation to a curve, the function of which purports to show that historically rising wages are always accompanied by high employment, or, stated differently, wages and prices rise and fall together. This curve, called the 'Phillips curve', spawned a new school of economics. Naturally, 'the curve' has had its refinements. The most cited at the moment is the Lipsey-Parkin thesis of two British econometricians, Richard Lipsey and Michael Parkin, which currently enjoys much esteem in discussions on whether or not to apply an incomes policy. Unquestionably this thesis underlies the error which the OECD committed in 1970 in recommending some unemployment to counter inflationary pressures. Enveloped in demand-mapping formulae, the Lipsey-Parkin thesis is that there is a triggering level of unemployment under which wage controls can be effective—1·8%. Above this crucial level, however, wage curbs are ineffectual and feed inflation rather than contain it.

Despite their current vogue, both the original and the later, more sophisticated versions of the 'Phillips Curve' bag of tricks manipulate aggregates which are no longer valid. Structural unemployment, the technological displacement function of modern investment, is largely ignored. The correlations, derived from a common-sense assessment of inflation and wage statistics, have become only partially relevant to the new variants of price pressures, wage packets and unemployment combinations in the economy. Trading off employment against inflation, in the imprecise undifferentiated manner of the Lipsey-Parkin model, will have no effect on the cash-flow pressures on prices or upon the structure and size of the technological portion of total unemployment. This technological component already accounts for nearly half the unemployment in the industrialized countries of the West, whilst in the underdeveloped areas it is almost the whole of the problem. The labour force groupings are imperfect substitutes for one another, and their dispersion and differentiation is growing under the emphasis on investments in labour-displacing technology. Under these circumstances nothing justifies the Phillips and Lipsey-Parkin postulate that wages are privileged or an essential source of inflation, and that trading unemployment for price stability is a sensible proposition in the complex economic reality of today.

IDLE MACHINES COST MORE THAN IDLE LABOUR

A consequence of the scales of modern plants, refineries, rolling mills and smelters is that internal fixed costs, extended globally, limit the possible responses of management to changing situations. Modern enterprises feel they are inexorably condemned to dynamic growth or to becoming targets for take-overs.

Such inflexibility of strategy limits the options available to management in responding to changes in other sectors of lesser priority. It is this capital elephantism, not monopolistic union power, which is destroying the 'time tested differentials' and disturbing the equilibrium between industries. A good example of this thinking is the 'plausible hypothesis' of Sir Frederick Catherwood, past Director General of the British National Economic Development Council. The new strain of inflation, he contends, has to have a common source, inherent in the circumstances of inflation-ridden countries. Such a common source, he suggests, might be the inability of large-scale enterprises, because of long-term fixed costs (commitments to protecting their share of the market from marauding competitors, to holding on to key dealers and distributors, to high costs of dormant productive assets), to fend off strong unions, especially at the plant level.

Because of the costs of fixed assets and sales networks, the annual loss from stoppages may go beyond the gains from fighting off the unions. On balancing the cost of strike against the cost of settlement, a company may find the weight coming down more firmly on the side of a settlement, he argues.

While the thesis itself is highly questionable as a decisive or general explanation of inflation, it probably has some degree of relevance as a secondary influence. More interesting than its central argument, however, is its move towards a structural explanation of inflationary pressures; especially in the opinion that, at the level of fixed assets in modern corporations, it is the rise in costs of unused capital and not the present and future wages bill that determines the point at which companies settle strikes.

A decisive failing of cost-push wages theory is that it is based on average labour cost and average productivity aggregates of the most dubious and qualified kind, which are totally inadequate for formulating policy.

Though still largely considered economic heresy, and rejected as mere self-serving rationalization by trade unions, there is, nevertheless, a growing admission that there might be some truth in such a proposition, even among some of the most impeccable and most representative institutions of modern capitalism. The chief economist of the mammoth, worldwide First National City Bank of New York stated in the Bank's *Economic Review* that he has stopped examining wages as a leading indicator for prices because he had found no statistical relationship which is any use for forecasting. The *Wall Street Journal* of 14 October 1970 reports that in the USA the highest prices are occurring in the industries 'where wages are the lowest, unit labour costs not even a consideration, and union organization the weakest'.

The more moderate price increases, it stated, are occurring in industries with the highest incidence of union organization and the highest average wages. It concluded that there was no especially close connection between the magnitude of pay boosts and price developments. This results from low unit-labour-costs and high productivity, which the third biggest bank in the United States, Morgan Guarantee Trust, has admitted are a function of high nominal wages and strong unions which have spurred investment in labour-saving technology.

DUBIOUS DATA

Awareness of the very limited value of national accounts and statistics as a basis for economic policy is also growing.

The *Guardian* published, on April 15, 1971, an article entitled 'Trade figures may still be wrong in spite of checks'.

According to the Department of Trade and Industry, it stated, the British export figures for March would:

1. contain two separate sorts of error, one which would tend to exaggerate the value of exports while the other does the opposite, neither of which can be measured yet, and may not be measurable ever;
2. be based on customs documents of which between 6% and and 8% are missing because exporters have broken the law;
3. contain uncertainties which HM Customs and the DTI would not be able to resolve until June at the earliest and about which they could not be finally certain for six months, if then;
4. suffer from distortions caused by the postal strike.

But the figures, whatever they say, would be taken as an important indication of Britain's economic progress.

This means that the elaborate and expensive arrangements that HM Customs and the DTI have made to ensure the accuracy of the monthly trade figures have failed in their object, if, in fact, the object ever was to ensure the accuracy of the figures. The statistical services of the United States government and certain economic models of US universities are incomparably more comprehensive and sophisticated than those existing anywhere else in the world. They have been assumed by the profane to have put a scientific seal upon economic analysis.

Policy-makers rely on such data to provide scientific backing for their political decisions. But recently, among specialists who ought to know best (like officials of the governmental statistical agencies and governors of the Federal Reserve Board), warnings are being heard that the data collected, and numbers compiled from them, are too limited, sampled and 'guesstimated' to be dependable for formulating policy.

The silly season for currency crises came early in 1971. Already in February and March, hundreds of millions, perhaps billions, of everything, but especially dollars, poured into Germany. The flight from the dollar was on and central banks began buying up dollars frantically. With speculation on the revaluation of the D-Mark, the crisis of the dollar became acute. The directors of the large central banks began warning the US that, unless it started to concern itself with its unfavourable balance of payments and put it in order, dire consequences could result.

It was with real embarrassment that the central banks learned in April, in a report prepared for an OECD working party, that their statistics which announced the crisis were in error owing to their unintentional but significant double counting of their reserves. The European estimate of US liability was double its real volume because the central banks have been depositing their dollar holdings on the Eurodollar market where they have been reborrowed by private companies. These in turn have converted them into domestic currency with the central bank, which again placed them on the money market. Such a circuit of the same dollars spirals reserves of dollars higher than they are. Thus the $11 billion US deficit in 1970 was financed at least to 50% out of reserves and swaps. Only about $6 billion was an actual dollar outflow. But the banks and central bankers were ready to push the panic buttons. The next step would have been to insist upon a wage freeze in the US to bolster exports and reduce the outflow. These false figures detonated the June 1971 currency crisis.

Perhaps the most poignant feature of the affair is that a large part of the responsibility rests with the staid, orderly and very responsible Bank for International Settlements (BIS) in Basle to which the central banks of the ten leading monetary powers adhere. It seems that it could not curb its penchant for profits, and invested $3 billion of member-banks' funds in the Eurodollar market, although its role is supposed to be to stabilize money, not to maximize profitability. Most of the protagonists in this organization are also leading exponents of the wage-cost push inflation theory. They are pressing for incomes policies and wage restraints, almost without exception, in their own countries. In view of such a glaring lack of professionalism and sloppy administration in their BIS operations, which helped provoke the type of crisis they are supposed to be preventing, one is entitled to entertain serious doubts on the wisdom and competence of their other national economic concepts and advocacies.

The reservation with which official statistical aggregates must be read was further dramatically illustrated by the report of a special working party of the Federal Reserve Board which seriously questioned the quality of the predictions of the White House on the American GNP for 1971. These predictions put the expected GNP as over $1065 billion. This figure, in the opinion of the central bank, is considerably inflated, and it suggests a shortfall or difference of between $20 and $25 billion. In supposing that these forecasts constitute the principal orientation of economic policy, the banks' experts declared, they can produce a catastrophe.

EXPERT OPINION

Sherman J. Maisel
Governor of US Federal Reserve Bank

Cautioning that very little is known about the money supply and what impact it has on the economy in the US, Mr Maisel said: 'He who points at a particular number as representing "the" money supply at a given time, and who then makes sweeping judgements about the direction of Federal Reserve Policy and its implications for the future, is bound to find that frequently he has built a fine analytical structure on shifting sands. . . . Knowledge of how changes in the money supply (and the aggregate measures of money and credit) affect the economy, are inexact.' Therefore when the Federal Reserve Board adopts a new policy stance it still has 'only rough ideas' of what will happen. 'The Federal Reserve Board's influence over the money supply is indirect,' Mr Maisel holds. 'The links between Federal Reserve actions and the decisions of others to alter the money supply are not fully understood. . . .'

Union des Banques Suisses (UBS)
(One of the world's major banks)

In its economic review for December 1970, after commenting upon consumer prices in Switzerland during that year, the UBS stated: 'The consumer price index is, however, not a reliable reflection of price trends. The monetary purchasing power experienced by the individual may deviate substantially from the averages shown by the index. Above all, the cost of living index is not a barometer of future economic trends. Rising consumer prices tend rather to be the result of economic strain that has set in earlier.'

In fact, not very much is really known of economic aggregates and their effect upon the billions of economic decisions which make up the system. This is as true of consumer behaviour, investment strategies, or productivity coefficients as it is of the nature and function of the money supply. Despite these explicit reservations, the aggregate numbers game is still played hard in most economic and financial departments of government in respect of inflation policy.

Perhaps the most widespread version of this game is the one which quantifies the inflationary spread between national productivity estimates and average rises in wages. Current figures used for industrialized countries run roughly as follows: national rises in productivity are given as falling in the 1·5% to 3·5% range; national industrial production is rising from 4% to 6% per year; nominal wages are estimated to be rising at around 10% to 12%; price inflation is projected at between 4% to 7%; rises in disposable free incomes in real terms for the average worker (after taxes, social insurance, premiums and consumer price rises are deducted) are projected at between 3% to 5%. The inflationary gap is supposed to be the self-evident spread between nominal incomes and average productivity resulting in higher disposable incomes which inflate consumer demand.

But these national averages do not factually reflect the pressures of wages on prices. Although they are difficult to estimate accurately, the comparative impact of wage increases in the capital-intensive sector (which accounts for the largest portion of GNP) upon the general price level is not inflationary.

In the United States, the national increase in average productivity of industrial output is running at about 3·2%, based upon the very crude measure of GNP divided by the number of man-hours worked. By comparison, average increases in productivity in the more capital-intensive industries is well above this figure. In fact, the figure of 3·5% a year is of no significance whatsoever in these industries.

In motor manufacture, the annual rate of increase in productivity in the last decade was over 6%, in rubber 7%, in chemicals 8%, in petroleum 9%, in pharmaceuticals 10%. These productivity advances have accompanied the reduction of relative labour costs per unit of output considerably below national averages. For example, in the motor industry it is around 20%, which would suggest that the price rise needed to reconcile a 10% wage rise throughout the industry would be roughtly 2%—assuming no changes in output, overtime, etc. In petroleum, where unit labour costs are well under 8%, the cost could be absorbed with less than a 1% increase in prices.

Calculated upon the value of sales, rather than volume of physical output, the unit labour costs all but disappear, and wage increases lose much of their meaning as constituents of price levels. Of course, all this assumes the maintenance of existing profit margins, both gross and net. For, in most cases, if consideration is given to the ability to absorb wage increases in profits in the modern expanding branches of industry, the entire case for wage-cost inflation becomes untenable.

There is no justification in these industries to reason in terms of the marginal utility of capital which posits that if return on investment falls below a certain point, capital would transfer out of the industry into another. Even at a lower rate of investment their level of earnings would exceed most alternative opportunities.

Price policy in capital-intensive industry is essentially a function of capital investments and the generating of planned levels of cash flow to finance them. To a very large extent this is really what big business is now about: corporate growth and expansion through maximization of retained profits and cash flow. This also explains why, instead of instituting a minimal 2% rise in prices to compensate for the costs of a 10% wage rise, the automobile industry has raised its prices three times during the past eighteen months by over 15%, and will certainly proceed to further adjustments during 1971; and it further explains why—despite enormous profits—petrol prices will rise and why chemical-process industries will raise prices in the face of falling unit labour costs.

IV. The Advent of Multinationalism

TOWARDS WORLD MONIES

The sixties produced the first international currencies and money markets. The Eurodollar, invented by the USSR and developed by Wall Street, expanded into a $50 billion pool. Eurobonds (denominated in dollars) amount to 2 billion annually and the creation of Special Drawing Rights (SDRs) (about $6 billion to date) within the International Monetary Fund helped to provide fillips to scarce world liquidities and reserves. The growth of total world exports to over $260 billion annually all but submerged the obsolete gold-exchange monetary standard. It revealed the fiction of sterling as an international currency and the fragility of the ratchety international monetary system—already a museum piece. The ratio of reserves to imports in the world fell from 74% in 1954 to less than 30% in 1970. But needs beget means, and new sources of liquidity were created to lubricate world trade and global profit-making, at least temporarily.

One of the side effects of this 'new money' is that national interest rates intended to meet the needs of domestic money and credit policies have lost a great deal of their autonomy and their effective range of float. The thrust of 'hot money' around the world; the hedging by world corporations against threatened currencies to protect vast, accumulated investment funds from erosion due to inflation or devaluation; the placing of billions of dollars, pounds, or francs on the short-term and 'spot' money markets by companies at high rates—these are other new, global monetary practices with which domestic management of money and credit must contend.

Corporate money management has become an important feature of modern finance. Some companies, like Ford, GM and the oil giants such as Shell and the Standards, have top executives in charge of placing their 'mise' on the *grand prix* hot-money circuit. The function of the corporate money manager is to follow markets and determine the best optimal mix for placing and recalling funds, and borrowing and investing short-term assets. These managers in effect put disposable money to work to earn the best yields until its number is called for the long-term input. An international gulf-stream of hot money, billions of dollars long and wide, is coursing around the national money markets of the world in the direction from low to high interest rates, raising and and lowering them continuously, usually in a contrary direction to domestic policy.

THE NEW INTERNATIONAL ECONOMY

The multinational company is creating the outlines of a genuine global economy. By 1975, nearly 35% of the Western world's non-US production will be accounted for by American subsidiaries or American-associated firms. Direct US investment in Europe rose from $6·7 billion in 1960 to over $21 billion in 1970—an increase of over 220%. In 1970, US corporations' subsidiaries increased their foreign plant and equipment expenditures by $13·2 billion—22%over 1969—and are expected, according to official US estimates, to increase it by 16% to nearly 15·3 billion in 1971. The larger part will be in Western Europe. In 1969 this expenditure amounted to only $10·8 billion and in 1968, to $9·4 billion. Since the end of World War II, American firms have established over 8000 directly-owned subsidiaries abroad.

During the last ten years, the book value of American investment abroad more than doubled, from $32 billion in 1959 to $70 billion in 1969 and $80 billion in 1970. By the end of 1971 US overseas investment will exceed $90 billion. In 1970 it rose by 22% to a record annual amount of $13·2 billion. In addition, about $1·5 billion a year has been added through reinvesting the profits from foreign subsidiaries. Foreign portfolio investment in securities is over $19 billion. Together, US foreign direct spending, reinvestment of profits and portfolio investments amount to around $120 billion. The sales generated by these productive assets is well over $250 billion a year compared to $40 billion in exports. By conservative estimates this is expected to reach $275 billion a year by 1972 while exports will rise to $45 billion. Tables

IV.1 and IV.2 summarize expenditures for various industries worldwide and for manufacturing investment in various regions and countries:

Foreign direct investment has been increasing at a rate of

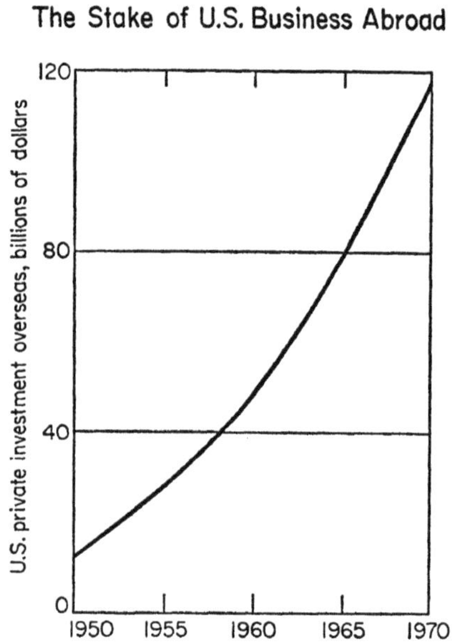

Data: Commerce Dept.
Fig. IV 1

TABLE IV.1. *Actual and Estimated Plant and Equipment Outlays by Industry (in $ millions)*

Industry	1968 (*actual*)	1969 (*actual*)	1970 (*estmtd*)	1971 (*estmtd*)	% *Change* 1971 1970
Manufacturing	4,191	4,976	6,803	8,137	19
Chemicals	1,208	1,118	1,354	1,570	16
Machinery	1,016	1,344	1,944	2,524	29
Transport eqpt	617	795	1,110	1,484	34
Other	1,349	1,719	2,375	2,560	8
Petroleum	3,311	3,640	3,916	4,693	20
Mining, smelting	1,035	1,132	1,294	1,534	19
Other	850	1,039	1,338	1,432	7
World Total	9,387	10,788	13,350	15,796	18

between 12% and 15%. On the basis of present trends this figure will rise to over 20% by the end of the decade. By contrast, GNP of the world's principal industrialized countries will increase at between 3% and 5%. This will intensify capital exports and exercise increasing pressure on

TABLE IV.2. *Actual and Estimated Manufacturing Outlays by Area (in $ millions)*

Area	1968 (*actual*)	1969 (*actual*)	1970 (*estmtd*)	1971 (*estmtd*)	% *Change* 1971 1970
Canada	854	1,036	1,222	1,303	7
Europe—Total	2,012	2,539	3,729	4,784	28
EEC	1,195	1,440	2,248	3,077	37
Belgium-Lux	153	111	176	241	37
France	306	338	557	690	24
Germany	423	607	993	1,560	57
Italy	166	181	260	326	25
Neitherlands	147	203	262	260	−1
UK	582	858	1,152	1,338	16
Latin America—Total	575	611	739	823	11
Argentina	71	95	152	149	−2
Brazil	186	186	190	265	39
Mexico	182	170	230	233	1
Afro-Asia—Total					
Asutralia	240	258	313	365	17
India	102	130	173	147	−15
Japan	227	268	429	531	24
South Africa	51	42	38	52	27
World Total	4,191	4,976	6,803	8,137	20

Source: US Department of Commerce

the world's monetary reserves, given that a growing part of total productive investment will consist of capital raised in one country and put down in another.

Total sales of foreign subsidiaries around the world arising out of $180 billion of book value assets is already over $100 billion greater than the total volume of world exports. The sales of American firms abroad are more than five times the value of the country's exports. It is expected to rise to nine times by 1975. American writer Ludwell Denny sums up the philosophy behind this drive: 'We are not without cunning.

We shall not make Britain's mistake. Too wise to govern the world, we shall merely own it.'

LE DÉFI EUROPÉEN

By 1975, just under a quarter of US GNP will be produced by European and Japanese firms. The great investment thrust of European enterprises in the seventies will be to the US, the world's biggest and most profitable market, thus complementing the efforts of American firms in Europe, including the US charter members of the European Common Market.

Foreign direct investment in the United States is expected to rise steeply as corporations abroad seek to enlarge their production and develop the organizational and financial strength needed to participate directly in the difficult but highly lucrative US market.

EXPERT OPINION

Herman Josef Abs
President of the Deutsche Bank and 18 other German companies
One of Europe's most powerful pillars of finance

'This workshop that is the Federal Republic of Germany only works and works without providing itself with adequate means to face the necessities of 1980 to 1990.' American firms implanted abroad, he said, produce four times more than the exports of companies located within the country. He declared that Germans should stop lending money abroad and create enterprises instead.

Giovanni Agnelli
President of FIAT

'US corporations are the only true European Multinational enterprises.'

M. Jacques Chirac
French Secretary of State for Economy and Finance

'We have a rise in the rate of industrial investment for 1970 in excess of 20%. France has been surprised by the international boom.

'All this because one didn't invest at the appropriate moment. One is precipitating therefore towards more investments in a period of high expansion, which serves to accelerate the overheating. . . .

'Equilibrium of the balance of payments and even its surplus is another necessity. It is in effect indispensable to constitute reserves in order to dispose of the necessary capital for our overseas expansion.'

By the end of 1969, such investment reached an \$11·8 billion total and for the first time had increased more than \$1 billion in a single year—after being only moderately short of this figure in 1968. A figure of nearly \$12 billion in foreign investment in the United States today may not seem important compared with a book value of more than \$80 billion for US private direct investment abroad. But foreign investment in the US is growing at a considerably faster pace at present than US investment overseas. These figures apply only to direct investments in manufacturing enterprises, and do not include portfolio or real estate investment. Today more than 700 US manufacturing enterprises are owned wholly or in part by almost 500 foreign companies. Foreign investments cover a wide spectrum of industrial lines. Particularly prominent is the chemical and pharmaceutical industry that has attracted large-scale Swiss and German investments. Historically, the largest aggregate investment has come from the United Kingdom, which accounts for about \$3·5 billion of the total and for about 107 enterprises in the United States. Canada is next with \$2·6 billion and 114 firms. The Netherlands follows, with \$1·9 billion and the distinction of having a greater investment position in the United States than American firms have in the Netherlands. Still relatively modest in aggregate terms, investment from Germany and Japan is increasing rapidly. Investment from Japan to date has been principally in developing sources of raw materials for its own industry, mainly in Alaska.

ICI announced in April 1971 that it was going to take over

the US Atlas Chemical Industries for \$163·9 million in cash. In announcing the deal, ICI Chairman, Jack Callard, said the merger was the most important single step ever taken by ICI in the Western Hemisphere. Especially interesting is the fact that the acquisition will be financed with funds from non-sterling sources, assisted by a consortium of American banks. Atlas, a speciality chemical and pharmaceutical firm, had sales of \$155 million in 1970. Mr Callard said Atlas provides 'the requisite strength in certain market areas and the very necessary management skills to complete the base from which major expansion will take place. This combination is an essential part of the policy designed to create a strong US company fully capable of developing on a broad basis from its own and ICI's innovations and research discoveries.'

The combined company is to be called ICI America Inc.

The Celanese Corp., another top US Chemical firm, is known to be discussing a joint venture with ICI to build a plant in Britain. John Brooks, President of Celanese, said that ICI now resells Celanese chemical products in England.

EVEN SMALL COUNTRIES HAVE GONE MULTINATIONAL

Long renowned as a host country for international banking and holding companies, Switzerland (which has 6700 holdings enjoying its tax-haven privileges) is less known for the fact that it has probably the most internationalized economy in the world. Beyond the extraordinary world-wide networks of its three leading banks, its *per capita* foreign investment, direct and portfolio, is over \$5000 compared with \$500 *per capita* in the USA. Nestlé, the giant food holding company, employs only 0·05% of its personnel in Switzerland. Hoffman La Roche, the world's largest pharmaceutical company does only 3% of its business at home. Ciba-Geigy is among the top five chemical giants and has only about one-fifth of its personnel in Switzerland. Most important Swiss enterprises have become world marketeers and have achieved a scale and importance greatly beyond the possibilities of a relatively small home market of seven million people to have nurtured.

In the sixties, the number of Swedish subsidiary companies abroad more than doubled, with mechanical engineering dominating more than half of the Swedish companies registered in foreign countries. As long ago as 1955 there were 260 marketing and 253 manufacturing subsidiary companies abroad. In 1969 investments in foreign subsidiary companies were more than twice what they were in 1968. At the end of 1969 there were 1806 Swedish subsidiary companies abroad, some manufacturing and some simply marketing

Little Luxembourg does a thriving busines in hosting base companies seeking to conserve as much income as possible from tax claims on profits. Among the thousands are many US companies like UniRoyal, Du Pont, General Motors, and also many from the other Common Market countries. Thus the European Common Market has its own built-in tax-haven. But, additionally, several important production subsidiaries operate facilities in the country as a basis for Europe-wide sales. In its own right, Luxembourg has the unique privilege of being perhaps the only industrialized country in the world whose total national income is surpassed by a single national enterprise. Acieries Réunies de Burbach-Eich-Dudenlarge commonly known as ARBED, partially owned by La Société Générale de Belgique, achieved revenues of 36,500 billion Belgian francs ($730 million) in 1970, which exceeds the total revenues of the country. A large part of these reserves are earned abroad.

CASE CAMEO

SKF

Sweden's largest multinational company, SKF, announced a slight profit decline for the parent company in 1970, from Kr. 67·6 million to Kr. 67·4 million ($13·5 million). But the President also announced its investment plans to exceed Kr. 2,500 million during the five-year period 1971 to 1975.

Planned investment in 1971, the first year of the plan, will amount to Kr. 600 million ($120 million), up 10%. This will be split up approximately between Sweden (Kr. 120 million—$24 million), the UK (Kr. 200 million—$40 million), and the balance outside Europe.

Direct foreign investments in Austria totalled net about Sch.2500 million ($100 million) in 1970, compared with Sch.1300 million ($50 million) in 1969 and Sch.1100 million ($44 million) in 1968, primarily from Germany and Switzerland, but also from the Netherlands, Belgium, the US and Canada. Nominal foreign investments more than doubled to over Sch.9000 million ($300 million).

While the foreign share of the capital of Austrian joint-stock, companies fell from 13·5% in 1961 to 12·6% in 1969, it rose from 46·8% to 56% of the limited liability companies. This contradictory trend, however, is due solely to the fact that foreign investors prefer the second category, which involves no obligation to publish balance-sheets and which can be set up with a capital of a mere $4000. In all, foreign investors have a majority holding in 127 joint-stock companies and 1275 limited liability companies, thus controlling about a quarter of the aggregate capital of all registered public and semi-public companies in Austria.

However, figures for nominal capital, which often exclude reinvested profits or loans from a parent company to a subsidiary, give an understated picture of the real size of foreign investment. The labour force clearly provides a more revealing index. In mid-1969, 111,000 Austrians, or almost 19% of the total industrial labour force, were employed in factories controlled by foreign capital. In other words, every fifth Austrian in industry is employed by foreign-controlled companies. Including all other branches, the number of Austrians working for foreign owners is about 150,000.

This becomes even more significant on a branch by branch breakdown, which shows that, in the electrical industry, 60% of the labour force is employed by foreign-owned companies, primarily by German concerns; in the chemical industry

24%; and in the paper sector 28%. Such growth sectors as pharmaceuticals, detergents, man-made fibres and plastics are dominated by foreign capital. In recent years the setting up of foreign subsidiaries and the takeover of Austrian firms have been particularly pronounced in the leather, clothing, textile, glass and paper industries.

Among the non-industrial branches, insurance is already subjected to what is claimed to be an 'intolerable degree' of foreign (primarily Swiss, German and Italian) domination, with the foreign share reaching about 58% of the total premium revenues. Such sectors as stores and mail-order houses, publishing and the tourist industry are also coming increasingly under foreign control.

During the 1960s there were striking changes in the league of foreign investors. In 1961 the US, with 28% of the foreign-controlled nominal capital, dominated the picture, followed by Britain, Switzerland and the Benelux countries. In that year, West Germany occupied a modest fifth place. Now, however, the Germans have become by far the largest foreign investors with 25% of all foreign holdings. Even in terms of nominal capital there has been an almost sixfold increase in German investments. The US has a stake of 20%, closely followed by the Swiss (almost 16%). By contrast, the UK has slipped from second to fourth place, with its share dropping from 15% to 9% of foreign investments.

The predominance of German investors is clearly due to geographical and language factors. Investments, however, are also influenced by the desire to increase trade with Eastern Europe. An investigation of the motives for American investments, which was recently undertaken by the Institute for Economic Research, quoted an American executive who stressed that 'for geographical and human reasons Austria is the best launching pad for exports to the East'. Out of seventeen trading subsidiaries of American concerns, eleven mentioned sales opportunities in Eastern Europe as one of the chief motives for going into business in Vienna. Many foreign companies also serve as centres for trade with Eastern Europe. The same motives are to some degree behind the setting up of subsidiaries by seven leading American banks in the Austrian capital.

Holland has been called a small, very densely populated country which has some of the largest companies in the world. Though the local market only consists of about 13 million people, three Dutch companies (Royal Dutch/Shell, Unilever and Philips) are among the world's fifteen largest—each with over $1 billion capital—no mean feat when one considers that the six largest of them equal the importance of the 300 leading French firms. The top four (the three mentioned above plus AKZO) have a total of 950,000 employees scattered around the globe in more than 300 plants and installations in fifty countries, only a relatively minor portion being located in Holland. Philips has only a little over 90,000 of its employees at home, the remainder of the 340,000 employees being located abroad. The Holland-based portion of Unilever's 330,000 employees is even less—only 20,000. AKZO's native staff numbers approximately 34,000 out of a total of nearly 100,000. Comparatively the most balanced in its inward/outward flow of capital, Holland's position in the UK and the USA is particularly strong, amounting to around $1 billion and $2 billion respectively. Overall Dutch foreign investment amounts to well over $4 billion and may even be as high as $5 billion. This would support a volume of direct overseas sales of between $8 billion and $10 billion, compared with exports of goods and services produced in the Netherlands of about $9 billion. The country's economy, therefore, is entirely dominated by the sheer size of the first four companies and through their joint structure, in the case of Unilever and Royal Dutch/Shell with UK divisions. In turn, Holland has been a strong centre of foreign investment, particularly in the Rotterdam area's attraction for petro-chemical and chemical firms: American, German and British investments in Holland increased by 140% between 1963 and 1968. At the beginning of 1970, American investment in Holland amounted to $1218 million. It has been running at about $290 million a year over the last several years and is expected to rise.

Foreign investment in Spain in 1970 amounted to 8·053 billion pesetas ($115 million), up to 87% from 2·969, official statistics show. Switzerland was the largest investor with 2·52 billion pesetas ($36 million), followed by the United States with 2·31 billion pesetas ($33 million).

Foreign share ownership in Italy's 663 largest publicly held companies totalled 1092 billion lire ($1·75 billion) on December 31, 1969, or 17·7% of the total capital of those companies, according to an official survey. Of the total 1969 list, 356 firms had no foreign participation at all. Of the 307 companies in which there was foreign participation, that ownership accounted for 26·4% of the registered capital. Swiss owners accounted for the largest percentage in 1969, with 36·5%; non-European investors (mostly from the United States) accounted for 24·5%, Common Market investors for 24%; and others (mostly from Great Britain) for 14%. But unquestionably the most *brutta figura* effect of all must be the seizure of Italy's pasta and ready-made spaghetti market by American firms. The giant American merchandiser of Italian-style packaged food products, Buttoni, is outselling Italian brands in Italy. W. R. Grace and Co., the fast-growing US multinational conglomerate (chemicals, services, metal, retailing, banking, transportation, plastics, etc.) has been rapidly acquiring European food and catering firms. Recently it acquired the French restaurant chain, Jacques Borel, and control of the chains of Salador in France and Eduard Malterne in Belgium. However, these are not as striking as its purchsse of Fratelli G. and R. Borilla Spa, the largest producer of pasta in Italy and in Europe, including sauces and pizzas, with a turnover of 50 billion lire ($85 million).

Olivetti is the largest producer of office machines in Europe, and the largest producer of printing calculators in the world. The headquarters in Ivrea, near Turin, controls a worldwide operation employing more than 73,000 people, fewer than half of whom work in Italy. Domestic sales in 1970 were only 22%, while 78% of total sales were made overseas. In Italy, Olivetti has 93 branches and 445 agents.

Outside Italy it has 30 different associated companies with 500 branches and direct sales agents. And even Cinzano, the vermouth producer, founded in 1757, has established factories and sales organizations around the world: nine factories in Europe, fourteen in North America, and another in Australia. Fiat, Pirelli, Montedison and the other giants of Italian industry all have more than 60% of their sales produced outside of Italy.

UK—Germany—France

Of the top 400 companies in the UK, around 65 are controlled by non-UK parents of which a dozen are amongst the 100 largest on the basis of turnover. Traditionally, the UK has the highest inward flow of foreign direct investment in Europe. US direct investments, which amounted to \$6·3 billion in 1968 represented 67% of the total book value of foreign assets at that time, of \$9·4 billion. US-controlled enterprises alone account for over 10% of total manufacturing, and provide just under 20% of the country's exports. Strongest foreign stakes are in auto, oil refining, chemicals, food and electrical engineering. The countervailing capital stake of the UK companies abroad exceeds \$20 billion at book value and represents half of the total non-American international investment. Annual UK overseas investments—including unremitted profits (\$700 million), portfolio investment (\$500 million), direct investment (\$105 million), oil (\$50 million)—reached \$2·3 billion at the beginning of 1969. ICI, Shell, Courtaulds, and the paper giants Bowater and Reed, all have extremely large foreign commitments with very numerous plants located around the world.

German foreign investment has lagged behind national growth and even capital exports. But the emphasis is swinging back (as in the case of Japan), as the Federal Republic will join the trend towards replacing exports through foreign investment. In 1960 foreign investment was only \$800 million; by 1970 it was over \$4 billion, an increase of over

500%. The rate of growth is expected to rise precipitously, particularly in North and South America.

West German industry invested DM 3·84 billion abroad in 1970 compared to DM 3·5 billion in 1969. Seventy-one per cent of this is invested in industrialized countries, of which DM 12 billion went to Europe and 29% went to developing countries. The chemical industry, with DM 5·26 billion, is the leading foreign investor, followed by electrical construction (DM 2·48 billion), automative industry (DM 1·9 billion) and mechanical engineering (DM 1·49 billion).

CASE CAMEO

Dr Ernst Von Siemens
President of the Board of Directors of Siemens

At the company's general assembly in April 1971, Dr Siemens reported to stockholders that sales in 1970 rose 19% to over DM 5 billion ($1·4 billion) and that the total projected for the two years of 1970 and 1971 of DM 14 billion would probably be achieved.

'Henceforth', he stated, 'we are going to further increase our production potential abroad. Siemens realized half of its sales outside the German Federal Republic although it produced only 20% abroad. In the future we are going to export more of our capital and our know-how instead of continuing to import foreign workers who already represent 20% of our internal work force. During the next ten years, personnel outside the Federal Republic of Germany will increase 50% and in the Federal Republic of Germany only 10%.'

Within certain branches, however, German firms are among the giants of their league. Bayer has 90 overseas plants in thirty-two countries, whilst BASF has thirty foreign plants. A couple of dozen account for over half of the total—these include Volkswagen, Daimler-Benz Siemens, AEG, and Mannesman. But the relative size of Germany's portfolio placements (notably in the United States) has been running at about triple the direct volume.

Foreign investments in Germany since 1961 amounted to DM 21·60 billion ($5 million) of which DM 10·61 billion is US and Canadian investment and DM 10·79 billion from the European continent. It is interesting that the amount of the Common Market countries' investment (DM 4·78 billion) was less than investment of the EFTA group (DM 5·98 billion). By branches of industry, petroleum was considerably in front (DM 4·45 billion) followed by the chemical industry (DM 2·45 billion), metal (DM 2·27 billion) and automative (DM 1·8 billion). Actually about 20% of the capital of German firms is in foreign hands. Of the 6500 largest stock companies, 1400 had majority or important minority foreign participation. Eight of the hundred largest are US-controlled, but their strategic positions typically accord them importance beyond their numbers: two have 50% of the petroleum market; two are among the top four auto firms (Ford and GM) with 40% of the market. US firms have one-fifth of the cosmetic business, and a third of the cigarettes, and half the razor blades.

France has a unique position in Canada. Both to penetrate the Canadian market and to benefit from Canadian advantages for entering the US market, about 110 French firms have been located in Quebec. Certain firms like Pechiney, Michelin, St Gobain, Rhône-Poulenc, or Renault have long had multinational locations. Renault, St Gobain and Michelin operate their international business through international holding companies in the tax-havens of Zurich, Fribourg and Basle, respectively. Directed towards the European countries for the most part, French foreign investments since 1966 have grown at a rate of five times higher than the growth of GNP. New important projects by Rhône-Poulenc, Michelin and Pechiney, when completed, will considerably improve France's position in the US market. France's small but growing overseas stake exceeds $5 billion. Inward investment turned upward with the lifting of the virtual veto of US investment imposed by General de Gaulle (supposedly to protect French industry from the Yankee predators), so that American investment in France is now around $2 billion. This is relatively less than in the other EEC countries where book values amount to $76 per person in Belgium, $69 in Holland, $52 in Germany and $36 in France. Next to the USA, Switzerland has the strongest position in French industry.

TABLE IV. 3. *American Subsidiaries in France, 1969*

Companies	*Employees*
Simca-Chrysler France	22·318
DBA-Bendix-Lockheed	18·524
IBM-France (Computer)	14·105
Kodak-Pathé	8·500
Idéal-Standard (construction industry)	7·000
International Harvester-France	5·898
Le Matériel Téléphonique	5·625
Esso-Standard	5·469
Ascinter-Otis	4·817
Sovirel (Glass)	3·796
Honeywell Bull	3·500
Mobil Oil Française	2·800
Caterpillar-France	1·797
John Deere	1·134
Esso-Chimie	692

In addition, other American firms have been long implanted in several branches of French industry such as food packing (Libbys), chemicals (Dow, DuPont), pharmaceuticals, land-moving equipment (Foster-Wheeler), photo (Kodak, Polaroid), and, recently, perfumes (Revlon), hotels (Hilton, Intercontinental), home building (Levitt), etc. In all, American investment in 1969 was 10 billion French francs ($2 billion), 40% of total foreign capital.

Besides direct spending, portfolio investment by Europeans in the USA has traditionally been high. Nearly 70% of total European investment in the US is portfolio investment, and only 30% direct. As a result there is near equality between combined direct and portfolio investment of Americans in Europe and Europeans in the United States. Despite the clamour against US take-overs of their industry, UK total combined investment in the US quite probably exceeds total combined US investments in the UK. Likewise, the amount of total French investment in the US is about equal to American investment in France.

CANADA'S SUBSIDIARY ECONOMY

Canada's political decisions are made in Ottawa, but its economic decisions—to a large extent—are made in New York, Detroit, Akron and Delaware. American ownership amounts to nearly 50% of all Canadian industries: nearly 70% of Canada's oil, 75% of petrochemicals and coal, 75% of its glass, 60% of its chemicals, 84% of rubber, 60% of the electric and electronic industry, 67% of its power, 65% of machine tools, and 95% of its auto construction. US influence over Canadian industry is much greater when consideration is made of the large number of Canadian-owned firms which operate as parts manufacturers, producers of intermediate or secondary products for American firms, and are therefore dependent upon them. It can be conservatively estimated that US influence extends over 70% of Canadian industry. More than a half of the total worth of the balance-sheets of Canada's 400 largest companies are in the hands of US firms. The addition of important UK, Dutch, French, German and Swiss firms located in Canada gives Canada the dubious distinction of having the most subsidiary economy in the world.

Capital movements in and out of Canada greatly condition the grip of official policy on the economy. US residents have a stake of around $125 billion dollars in Canada, mostly through stock ownership. Nearly 20% of the GNP of nearly $90 billion is contributed by US firms. To replace American investments, Canada would have to increase its proportion of Canadian capital spending (which is now around $13 billion) by nearly 25%, or about $3 billion a year more. National economic independence would have to be bought at the price of very high and sustained rates of inflation. In fact, the effect is even more onerous for the Canadian economy than is apparent from such figures. A serious drain on Canada's capital liquidity arises out of the repatriation of earnings through interest dividends, R & D charges and management fees, etc. From 1959 to 1968, such payments rose from $676 million to $1·38 billion. Extrapolation from this past rate shows that by 1980 Canada will be in the position (like many countries in the developing regions) of spending $3 billion a year (the equivalent of inflow of new US capital), just to service its debt to foreign owners. Under such circumstances there would be no net gain in the capital account; all that would happen is that a larger percentage of Canadian industry would be controlled by outsiders.

Thus, large amounts of retained earnings, achieved through higher prices and by technological unemployment in Canada, are being repatriated to the USA where they are consolidated in the International Division or global profit centres, and eventually re-expedited to one or another of the company's foreign operations.

In addition, most R & D is rationally concentrated in the large research divisions in the United States and contributes very little to the overall Canadian national effort.

The importance of the subsidiary segment of the economy deprives Canada of a vital part of its export base in manufactures. Subsidiaries' exports are restricted—in many cases forbidden (rubber, chemicals, glass, etc.)—by headquarters' global investment strategy. This is because profitable foreign markets for a company's products are covered by other subsidiaries.

This represents a serious handicap for Canada and a situation which could become critical by 1980. With a large majority of its enterprises excluded from multinational-scale operations, such expansion is limited to a very few Canadian-based firms. The result is that outside of banking there are very few Canadian multinationals for an economy of its size. When such multinational Canadian companies as Alcan, Domtar, Massey Ferguson, Seagrams, Polystar and a few secondary ones in service and insurance industries are ticked off, the list is almost exhausted. It could not be otherwise, for Canadian Standard Oil, Canadian Ford and GM, Canadian DuPont, Canadian IBM, Canadian Firestone, Canadian

International Paper, Canadian Michelin, Canadian ICI, etc., are already multinationals which are headquartered, managed and politically integrated in other countries.

The government is attempting to equip itself with more potent legal instruments for securing a greater sense of responsibility and commitment to the Canadian national interest from its alien corporate powers. But it will be a difficult exercise, not only because of the enormous economic power of the multinational corporations, but also because it means bucking the trend of modern industry. A better and more practical approach would be to facilitate the creation and growth of authentic Canadian multinational firms round the world. The belated establishment of a Canadian Development Corporation is a step in the right direction. It is certainly a more realistic response to the foreign companies in Canada than to attempt pressurizing them legally or to continue insisting upon incomes policies to control the inflation they help create. In such circumstances, an incomes policy is like attempting to stop a rampaging herd of elephants with a peashooter.

JAPAN TO GO MULTINATIONAL

Japanese industry has just begun a new policy of foreign investment. A government study revealed that, while the majority of important European and American firms do between 30% and 50% of their business overseas, only 2% of this on average is done in Japan. The intention is to make up this retardment as rapidly as possible. A large part of necessary capital will be raised on foreign money markets, so as not to disturb the rate of domestic growth unduly. Another important change of direction will be getting Japanese firms to raise a greater proportion of their capital out of retained earnings, currently averaging only 37% of industrial investment. To bring this figure up to the 60% to 90% levels of the US and Europe will entail a real, solid, long-term price inflation. Normally Japanese firms use employees' pension funds, savings and bonus plans and other social insurance programmes, usually provided at the company level, for their short-term, interest-free capital. This, plus the loans from their holding companies, has made 'debt financing' readily available. These sources supply nearly three-quarters of Japanese firms' total outside capital. Between 1956 and 1969, for example, Japanese industry put back earnings and loans into investment to the extent of 34% of the national revenue, as compared with 25% in Germany and 17% in the USA and the UK.

Japanese firms reported a decline in net profits in 1970 for the first time in nearly six years; these were down by about 5%. But, as elsewhere, sales were up—the 170 leading firms reported a 7% rise of nearly $6 billion. Investment is expected to fall only very slightly in 1971—if at all—from its record levels of 1969 and 1970.

Typical of the investment and financial practices of Japanese industry and the significance of net profit figures is the policy of Mitsubishi Shoji, which claims to be the world's largest trading company. Dealing in about 7000 products, it is the nerve centre of the Mitsubishi group of some forty-seven companies in metal goods and machinery, food products, petroleum, chemicals and, of course, the whole range of commerce and industry. Estimated total business is around 9% of Japan's GNP. The trading company's turnover in 1970 stood at nearly $10 billion. Its published net profits were a thin 0·2% on sales. However, its cash flow provided the means for loans of $60 million for iron-ore operations in Brazil, $200 million for participation in an oil project with Shell in Brunei, $50 million for loans to develop a chain of supermarkets, and so on. In all, Mitsubishi, according to one securities analyst, has committed something like 25% of its total assets—well over $400 million—in long-term loans and investment. Compared to this, shareholders' equity amounts to only 3·5% of total assets.

A greater share of capital investment is earmarked for foreign operations extending to all points of the compass: east to Formosa, South Korea, Hong Kong, to exploit the 'low-wage labour' available (low compared to Japan where rates are being raised by unionized workers); west to the USA and Europe to get into the high-wage mass consumption economies. It is also moving 'left' to China and the USSR and 'right' to Spain, Portugal and South Africa where Japanese corporation personnel are officially decreed as 'European' and not 'coloured' to avoid persecution under the laws of apartheid. In Budapest, a Japanese-Hungarian knitwear plant is being created by C. Itoh and Co., also a Japanese trading company, and state-owned Hungarotex Co. The factory would be owned by the Hungarian firm. The plant, including machinery, would be supplied by C. Itoh against repayment from production. To make up for lost time, joint ventures between Japanese and US and European firms are mushrooming. The attraction of this approach is that it provides immediate market penetration, distribution circuits and access to capital to both foreign partners who do not have to build up their operations from scratch.

A $100 million plastics factory and a battery plant using Japanese know-how, both in Belgium, form the spearhead of the new invasion by the Japanese in Europe. These two investments are part of current planning by trading and manufacturing companies to diversify Japan's export markets and lay greater emphasis on Europe.

Kanegafuchi Chemicals of Osaka, which is linked with the powerful Mitsui Bank, and the Mitsui Trading Company reached agreement with the Belgian government to establish a $100 million plastics factory in Geel City, in Belgium's Kempen area.

The Belgian government is encouraging 100% foreign investment with unlimited repatriation of profits, tax inducements, and low-cost loans to help boost underdeveloped parts of the country. Kanegafuchi and Mitsui Trading plan a wholly-owned subsidiary which could be Japan's first petro-chemical advance into Europe. It would produce synthetic-resin rigid sheets, pipes and irregular moulded products, as well as a polyvinyl-choride-reinforced synthetic resin made by Kanegafuchi, which is already being exported from Japan at the rate of 300 to 400 tons a month.

Matsushita Electric, Japan's most profitable firm and the leading electric appliance company, has agreed with Philips, the Dutch electrical giant, to establish a fifty-fifty jointly-owned factory near Turnhout, also in the Kempen area, to produce dry batteries using mainly Matsushita patents and expertise. The joint venture, called the Philips-Matsushita Battery Company, has Fritz Philips, head of the Dutch firm, as Chairman, and Masaharu Matsushita, the Japanese company President and son of the founder, as Vice-chairman. The company aims to sell all over Western Europe.

Other Japanese beachheads in its European invasion include: Mitsui (chemicals) in Portugal; Nisson Motors in Turkey; Kanegafuchi (chemicals) in Italy; Morenga-Mitsui (food) and Misshin Steel in Ireland; Koa Soap and Sanyo (electronics) in Spain; Terasoki (electrics) in England; and Dorina (sewing machines) in Germany.

South Korea has caught the eye of American and Japanese businessmen. Every week, numbers of them stop off in Seoul, the capital to check on the possibilities for investment.

So far, 88 US enterprises have started up, in industries ranging from automobile assembly to watchmaking. The American stake totals 120 million dollars, exceeding 60% of all direct foreign investment. More than two-thirds of these US dollars have gone into petroleum or petrochemical plants. Investors in this sector are Swift & Company, Skelly Oil, National Distillers & Chemical, Dow, Chemtex, Caltex and Gulf Oil.

Gulf was the first major US company to make a move in South Korea, helping underwrite the first petroleum refinery in 1963. Since then, Gulf has acquired the biggest interest by far of any foreign investor. Its equity now totals almost 50 million dollars in five joint ventures valued at more than 250 million. Outside of petroleum, most US money has gone into manufacturing, mainly in food, autos and electronics. Only in electronics is foreign investment making a significant contribution to exports. Firms in this field include Control Data, IBM, Motorola, Electro-Voice and Signetics.

What interests US investors most is the South Korean market of 31 million people on the threshold of prosperity.

Further advantages are low wages—about $40 a month in industry, one-fifth the Japanese level—and an able work force. On the minus side are official red tape, corrupt unions, and obligatory under-the-table payoffs to expedite projects. Japan is pushing into textiles, chemicals and electronics and it is known that German and Dutch firms are eyeing the area for future operations.

BRITAIN'S MULTINATIONALS IN THE COMMON MARKET

Much of the current discussion around the expansion of the Common Market might well be purely academic in its real significance to industry. Just as American enterprises have been among the first truly European multinational companies, with branches in three, four or five of the six countries, so British firms have already carved out a substantial stake by their direct investment. Dunlop's integration with Pirelli makes it half Italian. ICI's nearly two dozen branches are under the control of its ICI-Europe holding company in Brussels. Shell, Unilever (both half Dutch), Fisons, Beechams, Glaxo, Reed, Bowater, etc., are full members of the Common Market. As tariffs, border taxes, and other non-tariff barriers are only negligible factors in decisions to invest and produce abroad, these large firms would transfer investment to the Continent regardless of whether the UK is a political member or not. This is evidenced by the cross-investment which enterprises based in one of the Six carry out in the other countries, including Britain. Belgium, for example, invested $55 million in the other five countries from 1965 to 1969, and $45 million in Britain during the same period. French multinationals invested nearly $32 million in Britain during the last six years, compared with $155 million in the other EEC countries. Holland, because of the joint Dutch-British companies, such as Royal Dutch/Shell, Unilever, etc., has the largest European stake in the UK, amounting to around $1 billion compared with around $900 million investment in EEC countries. Total

British multinational investment in the Six amounts to over $2 billion (including banking). This represents sales of roughly $3 billion annually, compared with exports of around $4 billion. During the period 1959 to 1969 British industrial investment in the Common Market amounted to $625 million, a rise of nearly 75%. The rate of such cross-investment between the Six and the UK is about $500 million annually in both directions. This rate will accelerate, regardless of whether Britain joins the Common Market or not. The existence of such firms as Royal Dutch/Shell, Unilever, Lapointe-Solvay, Dunlop-Pirelli, Chrysler-Simca-Rootes, Ford (in the UK, in Germany and in Belgium), and Vauxhall-Opel-General Motors, represents a network years ahead of the political structure and far more important than the effects on agriculture and on exports and imports arising out of Common Market membership. Interrelated banking intensifies the industrial and financial penetration even further. It raises the question in fact whether the very concept of a regional market economy is still viable, conceived as an intermediate block between superpowers in the economic post-war era, in which economic thinking still ran long the lines of exports and imports, steel, heavy engineering, vehicles and coal mines. The question also arises of whether or not the multinational companies and their globalization of the market economy have not antiquated the economies of nation states. This seems particularly the case in the expanding, modern, capital-intensive segment of industry. There are good arguments and impressive statistics to support the argument in the affirmative.

For the last twelve years, the major part of EEC efforts has been devoted on the one hand to agriculture (the main sector where economies of scale, justification of the Common Market, are non-existent), and on the other hand to tariffs.

Now, the Commission has no illusions about the importance of these tariffs. It reported: 'The tariff duties are no longer the only, nor even the main instrument of commercial policy. In the new industries (which are called industries of advanced technology) foreign competition is expressed by investments and technology rather than by direct exports. The custom duties do not secure any protection on that score. On the contrary, their main effect is to attract more foreign investment. . . .' The result is that economic integration 'still hardly effects the structures of enterprise and the modern sectors of production', that is to say the principal factors which will govern the future.

Thus industry is not confining itself to the Common Market area, though it is reorganizing at a fast rate. But the setting up of powerful national groups will probably result in a return to national protectionism. For example, Montedison production represents 80% of the chemical goods market in Italy. How can one imagine that the Italian government, in the event that this company is threatened by the competition of a German chemical industry, could let it be jeopardized?

This tendency towards national withdrawal has two main causes. First, there is no power of decision in industrial policy at the European level, which is entirely in the hands of the enterprises; secondly, in most European countries and especially in France, public interventions are concentrated exclusively on the marginal industries and on the retrograde sectors—the head and the tail—to the detriment of the industrial body itself.

As a result, industry is not and cannot be a real operational concern of the Common Market, whose structure is made for processing the marginal problems of a receding agriculture (cheese, butter and cereals), not for electronics and chemicals. The large firms of the Six have not gone 'European'. They have (like the other giants) gone multinational. For the modern sectors of British industry, the political entry or non-entry is not a fundamental economic concern, just as it is of limited concern for the large enterprises of the United States, Switzerland, and Sweden which are all charter members of the Common Market. The 'European' enterprises have also outstripped the boundaries of the regional economy as they have outgrown their national cocoons and expanded into multicoloured, international butterflies. The major thrust of German metal industries will be to the East, not into Western Europe. Its chemical concentrations are heading to North and South America. Dutch retaliation against the UK would be unthinkable, given the dual citizenship of its largest firms and its important investment stake in the UK generally. As British and American firms use the hospitable, tax-haven advantages of Luxembourg, so European firms nestle cosily in Switzerland, through base companies and other tax-minimizing systems: French Michelin in Basle, French St Gobain in Fribourg; German Seimens in Zurich; Italian Pirelli in Basle—to mention only several of the thousands residing there. All of which seems to be deliberately ignored by spokesmen of British industry. W. O. Campbell-Adamson, Director General of the Confederation of British Industry (representing 13,000 firms), for instance, stated that the EEC's chief attraction was its plans 'for creation of a common industrial environment through the harmonization of taxation, standards, public purchasing, and company law'. This would allow for mergers of companies across national borders, something now difficult to achieve. If Britain stays out of the Common Market, he said, many British companies will face 'an unequal duel not only with giant American rivals, but with great European groupings as yet undreamed of'. Such opinion is quite antiquated and totally inconsistent with the economic facts of life. The fact is that of the one hundred companies which account for over 75% of British exports and of the fifty which conduct the largest part of foreign trade with the Six, all have direct investment, joint-ventures or other forms of multinational linkages with Common Market-based companies. Comments such as quoted above seem to miss the point completely that traditional import-export trade is not significant in contemporary practice, and certainly does not figure prominently for the future.

EUROPE: GATEWAY TO THE FAR EAST?

It has been clear for a considerable time that the growth of the multinational company was not properly understood in many economic and political circles. While paying lip service to the importance of the phenomenon, the practice has been to attempt to assimilate and deal with the problem within a traditional or national context. The emphasis has been on action by national organizations and policies to contend with this phenomenon, and not really to strengthen or better to create new international structures and counter-forces.

The same reasoning applies to regional organizations such as the EEC, EFTA, etc. The lesson of the multinational company does not seem to have been learnt. Instead of understanding that it has become 'intrinsically global', it is being assimilated within a context of regional area and given a regional nomenclature: 'European corporations', etc. But multinationalism is too potent a force for either national or regional containment. Its global power will shatter or at least enfeeble regional as well as national attempts at control either through politics or economics.

Many examples have been given of the American investment in Europe. Proportionately, there is almost as much American investment in Japan and the Far East. A new thrust of European investment in the US is taking place, especially in the chemical process industries. While less known, a European movement is also beginning towards the Far East. European firms, even if they become truly European under a new corporate law (which is most unlikely to see the light of day in real terms despite the constant propaganda of the Eurocrats) will move increasingly to Asia. Thus European firms will be producing in Japan and exporting unemployment to Europe, just as American capital exports goods and unemployment from Japan to the US.

Rising wages are encouraging a greater variety of the international companies to shift production from their home countries to Asia's low-labour-cost havens. For some years, US firms, especially electronics companies, have created production bases in Asia for exports to the US and other industrialized countries. European manufacturers are beginning to realize the advantages Asia offers as an export base, not only for light industrial production but also for highly sophisticated goods. Not surprisingly, West German firms are leading the way, but many other European firms can be expected to follow.

The German-Japanese camera scuffle

West German camera makers—once the world's leaders—have been steadily losing ground to their Asian competitors, even in their own domestic market.

Japanese camera imports by West Germany have been climbing at a faster rate than its own camera exports since 1962. Although the value of the average German camera exported is \$16, and the price of the average camera imported only about \$7, the extent to which Japanese cameras have eaten into the tightly-controlled German home market (about 6·7% currently) underlines the need for German camera-makers to become more price-competitive in all markets. Germany exported nearly two-thirds of its 1969 production of 3·9 million units, and imported 1·4 million units. Japan produced 4·8 million units in the same period and exported about 2·9 million (60%), while importing about half a million units. Most of the imports were inexpensive models made in Hong Kong.

Philips of Holland, Nestlé of Switzerland, ICI of England, Rhône-Poulenc of France, Solvay of Belgium, Wallenberg of Sweden, and a host of others have gone oriental. The trickle will become a tide, then a flood. This is another demonstration of 'globalization', which makes evident that national as well as regional considerations are obsolete. Such examples suggest that the Common Market or other regional groupings are concepts related to the pre-technological society and essentially are antiquated.

Two Asian countries are involved in the new developments, Japan and Singapore, and the 'migrants' are in the highly competitive camera industry.

For some time German camera-makers had been considering the benefits of Japan's relatively low costs plus technical expertise. Inflation and higher export prices due to the November 1969 revaluation of the D-Mark, coupled with the large labour input required in camera production, have finally convinced them that if they are not to lose more of their markets to Japanese camera-producers, they had better meet the competition on its own grounds. Already a small German company selling cameras under the Exakta brand name is having bodies and lenses manufactured by Niko Optical.

Now Agfa-Gevaert, the German photo-products division of the German-Belgian transnational group, is to have its new popular 8 mm. movie-cameras (both with zoom lenses) made under contract by Minolta Camera Co. in Japan. The initial order is for about 50,000 units. Minolta will not have any distribution rights on the Afga cameras, but will ship the cameras direct to Agfa distributors, the bulk going to Germany. First shipments from Japan were scheduled for early 1971.

The main reasons, according to German industry sources, why Agfa has gone to Japan are the low cost of labour, which is half that in Germany, and a lack of capacity at the company's works in Munich. The labour component involved in making the cameras made it more worthwhile for Agfa to contract out in Japan than set up a new plant of its own in, for instance, incentive-rich Belgium.

In Singapore the situation is a lot more revolutionary. Rollei-Werke Franke and Heidecke (Rollei), one of Germany's most renowned camera-makers, is establishing a manufacturing base for world exports for expensive 35 mm. reflex SLR models. Between now and 1972, Rollei will invest over $11 million in three subsidiaries: two wholly owned (one making cameras, the other optical parts), the third for as-yet-undisclosed purposes. Five years from now the company plans to have some 3000 employees in Singapore, 500 of whom will be qualified technicians, all working more or less under one roof on a thirty-acre site. An initial labour force of 1000 has just begun production on one type of camera and two kinds of electronic flash unit.

Besides Singapore's political stability and an incentive package (including fifteen years virtually tax-free), Rollei chose the island country mainly because labour costs are a sixth of those in Germany—a vital consideration since labour accounts for 50% to 60% of SLR production costs in Germany. However, since current productivity in Singapore is much lower than that in Germany, the effective saving in labour costs per unit will be only about 50%.

Despite healthy productivity gains—3% to 5% per annum—Rollei could no longer rival Japanese makers in export markets because of soaring costs (which have risen 22% since early 1969). About 70% of its production goes abroad, 25% of this to other EEC countries, 21% to the US. The recent devaluations and revaluations in Western Europe resulted in 35% to 40% price increases in such major markets as France and the UK.

To accelerate the start of production, Rollei is now operating in rented premises, but it will develop a thirty-acre plant complex on its own ground. At the moment some parts are imported from Germany, but later Rollei is planning to contract out production of various parts (mainly in Singapore itself but possibly in neighbouring countries). Initially, production will be sent back to West Germany; in a second phase after output reaches the projected 100,000 units a year, the plant will supply markets in North America, other parts of Europe, and Australasia. Significantly, once production reaches that level, Rollei is aiming for 10% to 12% of the entire world market, including that in Japan, despite the fact that Japan currently makes about 850,000 SLRs a year—about twenty-five times more than Germany.

THE TRANSFER PRICE

The view is growing that for large firms the interest in exports today extends largely to benefiting from transfer-pricing opportunities made possible through intra-company shipments. By manipulating the prices the parent charges for intra-company transfers among subsidiaries, profits can be managed so as to benefit from favourable tax laws by having the largest amount in tax-haven countries and a minimum in those with high profit taxes. Already nearly 60% of US manufacturing shipments are from the US parents to overseas subsidiaries. Nearly a quarter of UK exports are carried out under transfer-pricing conditions. Undoubtedly, a larger percentage still applies to French, Dutch, German and Belgian exports, but the practice is not controlled by the governments at all rigorously. Physical exports in classical terms are, therefore, already out of date, as management and capital rather than goods now cross frontiers, oblivious to and unaffected by tariff barriers and non-tariff restrictions on trade.

It has been predicted that certain advanced economies like the USA will transform themselves from export-oriented economies, to capital exporters exclusively. The deficits arising from imports will be made up in the earnings of their production abroad. Their new role will be to industrialize the distribution of credit on a global scale, and they will be concerned principally with the creation, distribution and raising the profitability of capital. An indicator of such a trend is the intractable and apparently permanent US balance of payments deficits. In today's global economy, such a deficit is no more a danger or a measure of the country's real trading position than the national debt of $354 million is to the economic solvency of a country with a GNP of $1 trillion. The price impact of such a transformation in the trade system on the other hand would be tremendous.

NEW MULTINATIONAL LINKAGE

It is not only the spread of the multinational corporation in itself which is important. The dynamics of the modern giant company produce new variants of international co-operation. Joint ventures are spreading more rapidly than in any period in history and new innovative, transnational linkage is being found to extend foreign penetration of markets. Two decades ago, nearly 75% of American foreign subsidiaries were wholly-owned. Today this proportion is only 40% because of the spread of joint ventures, and the rate is still falling. Standard Oil of New Jersey has over twenty jointly-owned companies, including ventures with Shell, Ugine Kuhlman, ELF Union and FINA rep. of France and Dutch Italian and Spanish companies. ICI, besides its vast network of West European subsidiaries under the holding company ICI Europe (situated in Brussels), has joint ventures with Solvay in Belgium, Rhein Chemie of Germany, H. P. Mallow of Denmark, Ciba of Switzerland, and several US companies. Shell maintains joint ventures with over twenty companies including many of its supposed competitors like BP, Esso, Texaco and Standard Oil of New Jersey. Over 65% of the joint ventures concluded by Common Market-based companies were with parent firms outside the Common Market. New types of venture—such as the worldwide integration of Dunlop-Pirelli operations, a UK-Italian linkage; and Solvay-Laporte, a Belgium-UK linkage—without merger or take-over, are taking place. The success of the Royal Dutch/Shell and Unilever cases, which are structured on the existence of two parent companies both inside and outside the EEC, will probably stimulate more such ventures. Agfa of Germany, a subsidiary of Bayer, which has vast ramifications outside the Common Market, and also Gevaert of Belgium have gone this route, as have Fiat and Citroën, SAS Airlines, and others. This means that where national governments raise legal obstacles against merging with foreign companies, the demands of modern growth devise new techniques for getting around them. Such enterprising linkages facilitate the utilization of sales and holding companies in tax-havens to minimize the overall tax bill and to rationalize the global strategy for accumulating and redistributing consolidated cash flows according to the investment plan. There is practically no important multinational firm which is not involved in such practices in one form or another.

To protect the value of their poly-currency, most multinational companies practice 'hedging'. Even if the foreign exchange markets appear calm, there are always some currencies weaker than others. The simplest method of insuring against a loss is therefore to deal in the forward currency markets, contracting to deliver a currency at a set price at a future date. If the currency is devalued, the profit on the sale should offset any loss from the devaluation.

Today's huge multinational corporations, with fixed investments, bank deposits and inventories in a number of countries, compute their exposure in a currency and buy a corresponding amount of coverage in the forward market. When the cost of forward cover gets too big, companies start playing with 'leads and lags'. This game entails reducing those assets in a currency facing devaluation, while building up assets in strong currencies. Facing a possible devaluation, for example, a subsidiary would speed up payments to the parent and borrow what money it needed locally (planning to pay back the loans later at the new, devalued rate). One rule of thumb is to have all accounts payable in the weakest currency and all accounts receivable in the strongest currency. And one aim of establishing centralized financial headquarters abroad, and of building computerized cash-management systems, is to improve a company's ability to play this circuit. More and more companies are devising increasingly sophisticated plans for use when currencies come under pressure.

While these techniques originate out of a corporate desire to evade and circumvent national claims on their profits, they rapidly become organic and permanent characteristics of a company's system of operations.

The extension of these fiscal channels has led inevitably to a parallel growth of multinational banking. The explosion taking place in the setting up of multinational banks and investment trusts which group leading institutions of five to ten different countries for the purpose of amassing and allocating funds among their global customers is revolutionizing the international money market.

Over 40 American banks operate in the Common Market. There are 30 in the UK alone. No fewer than 13,000 people are employed in the 200 foreign banks, including East European ones, located in London. The powerful Chase

Manhattan Bank has branches in over sixty countries. The Bank of America, the world's largest private bank, in as many. American banks are located in 104 countries with more than 2000 branches. British banking, with 5300 branches overseas, is nevertheless still the international queen of the industry. But the new rage is joint-venture banking. Already the important non-market banks are either buying up independents in the Common Market, joining with them in multiple ventures, or setting up new companies with separate identities to their parents: Rockefeller, Rothschild and the Vatican have formed a '3R Venture Fund' in Italy. The Société Francière Européene in Paris is owned by Barclays Bank of the UK, Bank of America, Banque Nationale de Paris, Dresdner Bank of Germany, Banco Nazionale del Lavoro of Italy, the Dutch Algemense Bank, and the Bank of Brussels.

THE RECEDING NATION STATE

The growth of the multinational business and of attendant multinational finance is unquestionably one of the most significant structural changes in modern economic history. Before its concentrated power, the ability of the nation state to control its own economic system is being put into question. Already the nation state, while it continues to reign, seems to have been deprived of its power to govern. It is steadily being sapped of its power over its economy, for example, in its helplessness to contain inflation. The odds against its not succumbing in a slow but steady retreat are very long indeed.

EXPERT OPINION

George Ball, (Banker)
Former US Under Secretary of State and US Ambassador to UN

In an essay on the cosmo-corporation, he asked 'How can a national government make an economic plan with any confidence if a board of directors meeting 5000 miles away can, by altering its pattern of purchasing and production, affect in a major way the country's economic life?'

In terms of either accumulated assets or annual production, the multinational companies are shaping up as formidable rivals to nation states, as the table on p. 105 indicates.

On the basis of output, among the top 100 countries and enterprises with a volume exceeding $2 billion annually, 54 are business enterprises and only 46 are countries. General Motors' turnover of over $24 billion makes it the fifteenth economic power in the world, slightly under Spain, Sweden and Holland but ahead of Belgium, Argentina and Switzerland. Standard Oil of New Jersey and Ford produce more in monetary terms than Pakistan, Denmark and Austria. Given that multinational investment is moving at a faster rate than economic growth (about two to three times), the relative weight of enterprises to states will expand in favour of the enterprise. When the associated banking and fiduciary institutions and the interlocking directorates through which many firms are linked are added, the positions of all the firms go up several steps and that of most governments would be lowered.

However, as impressive as these statistics are, they do not fully illustrate the true challenge of the multinational company to political power. This heightened challenge comes from two vital characteristics: its inherently international nature and its global mobility. In the seventies the multinational company will truly come of age. From their beginnings as large national companies doing some business abroad in the first stage, they develop into firms primarily related to their home base, but doing an important part (but still less than half) of their business overseas in the second stage. Finally, they will become intrinsically international with more than three-quarters of production and sales carried on outside of any one country. Strategies planned at headquarters for personnel, and above all for investments and sales, will be conducted on a planetary basis. Their

TABLE IV. 4. *The 100 top 'GNPs' in 1969 (excluding communist countries and international merchant banks)—in millions of dollars*

1.	United States	931·4	35.	CHRYSLER	7·0	69.	Algeria†	3·2
2.	Japan	164·8	36.	South Korea	7·0	70.	Morocco	3·2
3.	West Germany	153·7	37.	MOBILE OIL	6·6	71.	SWIFT	3·1
4.	France	137·8	38.	Thailand	6·3	72.	South Vietnam†	3·1
5.	United Kingdom	108·6	39.	Colombia	6·1	73.	MCDONNELL DOUGLAS	3·0
6.	Italy	82·3	40.	Indonesia*	6·0	74.	UNION CARBIDE	2·9
7.	Canada	73·4	41.	UNILEVER	6·0	75.	BETHLEHEM STEEL	2·9
8.	India	39·6	42.	TEXACO	5·9	76.	BRITISH STEEL	2·9
9.	Brazil	39·4	43.	Egypt*	5·7	77.	HITACHI	2·8
10.	Australia	29·9	44.	Chile	5·5	78.	BOEING	2·8
11.	Mexico	29·4	45.	ITT (+GRINNEL)	5·5	79.	Libya‡	2·8
12.	Spain	28·7	46.	Portugal	5·4	80.	EASTMAN KODAK	2·7
13.	Sweden	28·4	47.	New Zealand	5·3	81.	PROCTER & GAMBLE	2·7
14.	Netherlands	28·4	48.	Peru	5·1	82.	ATLANTIC RICHFIELD	2·7
15.	GENERAL MOTORS	24·3	49.	GULF OIL	4·9	83.	NORTH AMER. ROCKWELL	2·7
16.	Belgium-Luxemburg	22·9	50.	WESTERN ELECTRIC	4·9	84.	INTERN. HARVESTER	2·6
17.	Argentina	19·9	51.	US STEEL	4·7	85.	KRAFTCO	2·6
18.	Switzerland	18·8	52.	Israel	4·7	86.	GENERAL DYNAMICS	2·5
19.	South Africa	15·8	53.	Formosa	4·6	87.	MONTECATINI EDISON	2·5
20.	STANDARD OIL NJ	15·0	54.	STANDARD OIL OF CALIF.	3·8	88.	TENNECO	2·4
21.	FORD MOTOR	14·8	55.	Malaysia	3·7	89.	SIEMENS	2·4
22.	Pakistan	14·5	56.	LING-TEMCO-VOUGHT	3·7	90.	CONTINENTAL OIL	2·4
23.	Denmark	14·0	57.	DU PONT	3·6	91.	UNITED AIRCRAFT	2·3
24.	Turkey	12·8	58.	PHILIPS	3·6	92.	BRITISH LEYLAND	2·3
25.	Austria	12·5	59.	SHELL OIL	3·5	93.	Kuwait	2·3
26.	ROYAL DUTCH/SHELL	9·7	60.	VOLKSWAGENWERK	3·5	94.	DAIMLER-BENZ	2·3
27.	Norway	9·7	61.	WESTINGHOUSE ELECTRIC	3·5	95.	FIAT	2·3
28.	Venezuela	9·7	62.	STANDARD OIL (Indiana)	3·5	96.	FIRESTONE	2·3
29.	Finland	9·1	63.	BP	3·4	97.	AUGUST THYSSEN-HUTTE	2·3
30.	Iran	9·0	64.	Ireland	3·4	98.	TOYOTA	2·3
31.	Greece	8·5	65.	GEN. TEL. & ELECTRONICS	3·3	99.	FARBWERK HOECHST	2·3
32.	GENERAL ELECTRIC	8·4	66.	ICI	3·2	100.	BASF	2·2
33.	Philippines	8·1	67.	GOODYEAR TYRE & RUBBER	3·2			
34.	IBM	7·2	68.	RCA	3·2			

(Source: *Vision*, Paris.) * 1967. † 1968. ‡ 1969 Estimation

character like their currency and management will be global and without decisively binding ties or commitments to any one state or combination of states. Politically they will disregard the structure of the regimes and function easily and profitably in all hospitable systems whether they be democratic or totalitarian, capitalist or socialist, civilian or militaristic, developed or underdeveloped.

PRESSURE ON THE 'DEVELOPING' COUNTRIES

While India seeks foreign aid to help its development, it is confronted with two new forms of economic problem. One is the importance of foreign enterprise in India. At present, there are between 170 and 200 foreign trading firms in poor, hungry India, operating in the major branches of industry. The government felt constrained to tighten the curbs on their operations somewhat, especially as they are trading operations (as distinct from manufacturing investment) which represented an outflow of foreign exchange. It consequently placed restrictions upon the repatriation of profits and other types of remittance.

But an even greater drain on India's scarce foreign exchange and a threat to its industrial development, has been the growth of Indian private investment abroad. Some thirty major projects in engineering, paper and diesel-engine manufacturing are being carried out by the large Indian firms such as Tata, Birla Industries, etc. Tata Enterprises has entered the Argentine chemical industry. It is building a 200,000-metric-tons/year Solvay-process sodium-carbonate plant near Mar Chiquita, a 770-square-mile salt lake in Cordoba province (about 350 miles north-west of Buenos Aires). Initially, Tata will own 69% of the $35-million project. The provincial government, which owns the remaining interest, has an option to acquire an additional 21%. Given the limited consumer markets at home, a large company in a developing economy comparable to large firms in small industrialized countries feel obliged to go overseas in order to expand and grow. Thus, the anomaly arises that while the country seeks capital for its own development, its national private firms are impelled to spend capital abroad in order to prosper. This will become a universal problem as such firms acquire larger dimensions, no longer compatible with the restraints of the local markets. Therefore, not only will developing countries have to worry about servicing the growing debt of their foreign assistance loans, but also of the outflow of local earnings to finance foreign investment. They will be caught in a new type of capital squeeze from both sides.

INFINITE VARIETY

Thus geographically, ideologically, and culturally, the multinational company will seek a position of neutrality and avoid involvement, for too visible an identification with a particular political system exposes its subsidiaries to retaliation in the rival countries. Lauding apartheid would hurt GM, ICI, or Bayer in other countries of Africa and at home; attacking it or discouraging it would not be profitable in South Africa. Opposing communism in some areas openly and aggressively would not be appropriate for firms with extensive stakes in Eastern Europe. Benign disinterest will be the profit-posture of the multinationals to the political and social values of civil rights, personal freedoms, democracy and economic justice.

Most of the large firms today have operations or base companies in Spain, Greece, South Africa, Portugal, the junta countries of South America, at least one of the communist countries, besides those in the democratic countries.

A striking example of the power of the multinational company to penetrate the political policies of nation states is their expanding operations in both the Arab countries and Israel despite the state of war and the existence of an Arab boycott. American corporations such as IBM, Xerox, Chase Manhatten Bank, and Standard Oil operate in Egypt and Israel.

The general Tyre and Rubber Company manufactures tyres in both Morocco and Israel. The French tourist company, Le Club Mediterranée (of which Baron Edmond de Rothschild owns 35%), operates vacation camps in the Arab countries as well as Israel. Hilton and Sheraton Hotels are situated in Jerusalem and Tel Aviv as well as Cairo, Kuwait and Beirut.

Britain's Leyland automobile corporation is an important supplier of Land-Rovers to the Egyptian armed forces and they are used also by the Palestinian commandos, in spite of the fact that the corporation has two assembly plants in Israel.

Of course, all this could just mean the end of party politics as we have known it, which, if it can be achieved within a framework of individual freedom and new forms of participatory democracy, might not be a bad thing at all.

The second characteristic of the multinational concern is its adaptability and geographic mobility. No matter how a modern state strives, it cannot divest itself of its territorial limitations. It can extend them by conquest or commerce, but it cannot strip itself of its territorial definition, without ceasing to be a state and surrendering its power. Expansion through ideology on the Russian model is now beginning to regress, with the odds in favour of national states of communism emerging within a decade. The multinational company has no territorial definition. Traditional horizontal, surface space is of no interest to it. Outer space or scientific space is. Its communications will be over micro-wave channels, relayed by orbiting telecommunications satellites, and the data transmitted will be processed by co-ordinated global computer networks. As it is able to locate its personnel, plants and facilities anywhere in the world and design its distribution and financial systems according to global criteria, its options will always be numerically superior to the pressures or restrictions which territorially restricted institutions, including nation states, can muster. If governments refuse their conditions, the multinationals can pack up and go elsewhere. Penalizing the multinational company through high taxes merely means a shift in corporate nationality and amassing the profit surplus out of the government's reach. These advantages of superior options are being enhanced and multiplied by advances in science and technology. Modern industrial processes, automation, very sophisticated investment strategies and enormous rises in productivity are freeing the multinational from conventional restaints. Labour skills, distribution and transportation facilities, banking facilities, tariffs, taxes, etc. are no longer the drag upon the international company's orbital operations they once were, and they are fading fast. The importance of the obstruction caused by each individual factor in the overall programme is therefore subsiding rapidly. Very high value per ton, pound or unit of output reduces the relative weights of these costs in the end price. The advantages of low labour costs and low taxes in base-company tax-haven headquarters more than offset other comparative geographical advantages which (according to theory) used to determine the way in which a company optimized its international trading activities. Present trends point to a quickening of the tempo of change favouring globalization. It will carry the multinational company with it, and leave the nation state, along with all other national or territorially circumscribed institutions, woefully behind. The control functions in the modern enterprises and even more so for those of the future will be fluid and multi-formed. The nerve centre will probably be a temporary command post in a tax haven on an island. Compared to this the cumbrous, fixed, massive power of nation states will become impotent and dinosaur-like.

In the confrontation with the static power of the nation state the multinational company has become a creative, dynamic institution. It will spend a great deal of money and mind in devising legal evasions of national restraints upon its growth. For example, in countries where rising nationalism threatens established old-time imperalist interests, like US companies in explosive Latin America, or British companies in the fading Commonwealth, the ruse will be to joint-venture a new entity by bringing in partners from other countries, so spreading the political risk and simultaneously increasing the protection. The oil companies have done this in regard to OPEK oil. When an Arab country takes on the consortium of five or six different companies, it also takes on the combined political backing of their governments. Under such conditions it is difficult to raise charges of colonialism and Yankee or British imperalism.

In the face of rising nationalism and expropriations by military juntas (who were Washington's surest guarantees a few years ago), US companies are planning investments in Latin America, but settling for less than 100% ownership of their properties—less than 50% in some cases.

A few years back, for example, Dow Chemicals announced plans for a $100-million petrochemical complex at Bahia Blanca in Argentina, and gave every indication that the company planned to go it alone. But since then the Argentine government and private Argentinian interests have come into the act. Dow will have only a 25% stake in Procegas, a company that will build a gas-extraction unit at Bahia Blanca to process natural gas from the government's Gas del Estado. Probable other partners in the venture include: Gas del Estado; Fabricaciones Militares, the Argentine army's industrial company; and Perez Company, a private local firm.

Dow's operations may also be in jeopardy in Chile, where President Salvador Allende has said his country will nationalize basic industries. The company's Chilean affiliate, Quimica Plastica, is owned 70% by Dow, and 30% by the government's Petroquimica Chilena. Both partners have agreed to sell 10% each to private Chilean interests when the operation becomes profitable.

Even though Brazil's policy is more flexible than that of other South American countries, some US firms will prefer a minority position in new ventures. For example, Du Pont, which usually prefers to steer clear of joint ventures, has accepted a 45% interest in Salgema Industrias Quimicas, a projected $64-million chlor-alkali complex at Maceio in north-east Brazil. The plant is expected to turn out about 220,000 m.t./year of chlorine, and 250,000 m.t./year of caustic soda, by 1973. Design capacity is double those amounts. Du Pont's likely partners are Banco Nacional Desinvolvimento Eeconomico (45%) and Euvaldo Freire de Carvalho (10%).

BANKING GOES GLOBAL

The futility of pinning national labels on banks today is made clear from the fact that out of twenty leading multinational banks created in Europe (most with headquarters in London) twelve have one or more US partners and of the dozen multinational private banks which will completely dominate the world's financial markets by 1980, all will have American, European and Japanese partners.

One of the latest deals involved the US INA Corporation buying a 10% interest, valued at $30 million dollars, in the French Suez Company. The Company operated the Suez Canal before the waterway was nationalized by Egypt in 1956. Since then, the firm—based in Paris—has diversified. It controls banking, insurance and industrial companies. Directly-owned assets of the Suez Company are put at $600 million. Its control extends over assets worth more than five times this amount. INA lists assets of more than $2 billion in insurance and investment-banking operations. The US firm and the Suez Company plan close working ties. Their aim is 'to further each other's expansion in finance and industry'. Almost at the same time, a mammoth financial multinational operation was mounted, comprising major commercial banks in four countries. The partners included Chase Manhattan of New York, National Westminster of Britain, Royal Bank of Canada, Landesbank Girozentrale of West Germany. In London they are setting up three companies bearing the name 'Orion'. One will handle investment banking, the second medium-term lending, and the third co-ordination and planning. The recently formed Atlantic International in London has major Italian, French, Dutch, British and American banks as shareholders.

A particularly heterogeneous amalgam of multinational

mixes is a new vehicle put together out of the most improbable parts. To be called USSIFI, it involves Italy's Fiat Motor Company, the United States Corporation (the world's largest steel company), three major financial houses including Italy's Instituto Finanziaro Industriale (IFI) which is state owned, Switzerland's Alcareg and France's Lazard Frères. The latter is only the Gallic branch of one of the major commercial banks of the world, as important in the UK, USA and Italy as in France. It is the financial advisor of the Shell Oil Company and is a member of the Board of Fiat. The seat of the company will be located in hospitable, tax-free Luxembourg, from where it will exploit worldwide investment opportunities in real estate, construction, tourism, travel and other fields.

Every day, new joint ventures involving European, British and American banks are reported. In this profound restructuring of world banking concepts, conventional opinions on money rates, interest, national investment and fiscal policies simply become meaningless.

EXPERT OPINION

Sir Leslie O'Brien
Governor of the Bank of England

'Our banking system is a healthy one, operating in conditions conducive to its growth and increasing strength. This is all the more important because of the increasingly international character of the London banking community. Over the past fifteen months some twenty foreign banks have opened offices in London, and the pace shows little sign of slackening despite the rise in the cost of suitable premises and of the technical specialists required.

'In recent years many banks, as we all know, have come here primarily to seek international business, particularly in the Euro-currency markets. During this period such business has been the major growth point in the City's financial activities, and there are a number of reasons why we welcome this development.'

M. Jean Terray,

Compagnie Financière de l'Union Européenne and Banque de l'Union Européenne

President of a large European financial group operating through banks and funds in many countries, and through a holding company, 'Interunion', in the tax-haven of Curaçao, with a total balance-sheet worth over $600 million and a turnover in the billions of dollars range, M. Jean Terray stated in an interview recently, 'Within ten years all in the important banks will be international.'

CAPITALIST INVESTMENTS PRODUCING HIGH COMMUNIST CASHFLOW

Lenin declared in 1920 that he saw no reasons whatsoever 'why a socialist state like ours cannot have unlimited business relations with capitalist countries'. He was obviously thinking in terms of trade and exchanges of goods, and he would be pleased with the growth in East–West trade today. Most industrial countries are expecting trade with Eastern Europe (notably with USSR) to increase fourfold by 1980. But is not equally certain that Lenin would have been so pleased with a new trend which seems about to explode the doctrinal content of his socialist state, just as it is destroying the classical distinctions between capitalism and socialism. Both ideologies are undergoing 'profitability' transplants, after which they will never be the same again—if their grafts take, they will have to maintain doctrinal subservience to the overriding imperatives of capital investment.

Just as in the West, it is not goods which are going over the borders, as in the time of Lenin, but capital and technology. Huge investments by private capitalist firms are bringing capital goods and equipment into the East. US technology is pouring in, either through foreign subsidiaries or indirectly through other foreign firms like the Japanese. The amount of such capital transfers even at current levels will have a significant impact on the available capital in the direction of making it even scarcer. While this may prove advantageous to the capital goods industries, the net effect will be inflationary, because the investment will not produce more consumer goods on the home markets, except for cheaper imports which will make things more difficult by replacing domestic consumer output.

The new East–West deals being worked out are different in that they entail the creation of joint doctrinally-hybrid enterprises, part-communist government and part-private capitalist. Eastern managers are hurriedly attempting to acquire Western management know-how. The ILO conducts extensive programmes for transferring advanced US management techniques to the East. Soviet managers are even studying the famous case-method of the Harvard Business School, whilst private management consulting firms (including US ones) do a profitable trade in organizing joint East–West management seminars in the USSR, Hungary, Poland, and so on. A big feature of the training is to polish up management concepts of efficiency, and above all such investment planning techniques as discounted cash flow. Soon Eastern management, like their Western counterpart, will be lamenting the wage-cost push of inflation and the need for more rigorous incomes policies and restraints on consumption than those applied up to the present by force.

A symbol of the increasing rush to capitalize on communism is a new venture being negotiated by Cleveland financier, Cyrus Eaton. It is for a $40 million investment in a new East European tyre plant on a fifty-fifty joint-venture basis. The Western half will be located in Switzerland with the communist state partner owning and operating the plant. The interest of the deal is that the Swiss company will have the right to market its tyres everywhere in the West.

'This enables the Eastern country to earn hard currency, and', as Mr Eaton explains further, 'because of lower labour costs the venture can sell tyres cheaper than Western companies can.' The plant in the East will sell the tyres to the marketing subsidiary at 'cost', thus leaving profits from Western sales in the joint marketing subsidiary. Many fifty-fifty partnerships are presently under discussion for the transfer of Western capital and technology to the East: French Pechiney is negotiating with Hungary to set up aluminium-based industries; US oil companies are seeking to put up refineries in Romania (UK has just opened up its markets to Soviet crude oil refined through BP).

Even the commercial relations between Spain and the communist countries have been quietly extended, despite the apparent antagonism of official policy. In April 1970 Poland signed a five-year economic and technical agreement with Spain. Early in 1970, Polish coal was sent to Spain while Asturian miners were on strike. Spanish Pegaso-LKW trucks are being delivered to Poland (250 to date and more projected). Other commercial agreements have been concluded between Spain and Bulgaria and Czechoslovakia. A secret accord dating back to 1967 gives Soviet and Spanish ships reciprocal rights to use each other's ports as well as agreeing the delivery of half a million tons of Soviet petroleum to Spain. Trade between Spain and Yugoslavia has reached the point where the Spanish government has been permitted to establish a consulate in Belgrade.

In fact, Yugoslavia is experiencing a 'boomlet' of Western investment. Some of the biggest ventures are in motors. Italy's Fiat has invested $36-million, Germany's Daimler-Benz and Kloeckner-Humboldt-Deutz are completing arrangements to build trucks; while Ford, Chrysler, France's Renault, and British Leyland are all exploring or negotiating joint ventures.

In the three years which have elapsed since the introduction of legislation to open Yugoslavia to foreign investment, foreign companies have contributed about $70 million in equity in twenty-nine joint ventures. Italy, West Germany and, recently, the US have been the leaders. A first UK joint venture was formed in April 1971 between the Dunlop Rubber Co. and a 51% parent Yugoslavian enterprise for the production of braided base. Dunlop's initial investment amounts to $675,000. Output is slated for Eastern European outlets as well as for home markets.

The London-based International Investment Corporation for Yugoslavia (IICY) played an active role in assisting Dunlop and FADIP during the negotiations, and contributed 19·3% of the fixed investment. The IICY was set up in early 1970 to promote joint ventures between foreign companies and autonomous Yugoslav enterprises in industry, mining, tourism and agriculture. Its charter shareholders are fifteen leading Yugoslav banks, the International Finance Corporation of the World Bank, and forty banks from Western Europe, the US and Japan, including the Bank of London and South America Ltd, Barclays Bank Ltd and Lazard Brothers.

The projects which IICY have completed, or on which it is now working, are principally joint ventures in the vehicle and associated industries for which a rapidly expanding market exists in Yugoslavia; in the non-ferrous mineral and pulp and paper sectors, for which natural resources are available; and chemicals and petrochemicals, for which a substantial domestic market has developed. Projects in other manufacturing industries are planned.

Projects range from those with capital costs below $5 million to ones in the mining, aluminium and petrochemical industries with capital costs amounting to $100 million and over.

Joint ventures are just the latest development in the evolution of East-West business ties. For some years West European companies have been making 'co-production' deals with communist enterprises as a means of tapping the supply of low-cost labour in Eastern Europe. Under a co-production arrangement, a Western company provides technology and machinery to build or re-equip a plant in a communist country, and takes part of the production in payment. Some of the biggest names in capitalism are involved: Fiat, Renault, Pirelli, ICI, Rockefeller, IBM, Shell, SKF, etc. Customers would be surprised if they knew that the products they were buying with the company's label were actually manufactured in Eastern Europe.

A famous case is one of the few US companies with such

a set-up in Eastern Europe—Simmons Machine Tool Corp., of Albany, NY. Czechoslovakia's Skoda makes big machine tools to Simmons' specifications, and Simmons sells them in the US under the Simmons-Skoda name.

An even more elusive form of East-West business link is being established with the purpose of penetrating markets in third countries. Austria's Simmering–Graz–Pauker, for example, is collaborating with a Polish enterprise in building a sugar factory in Greece. The Poles will supply equipment, and the Austrians will put up the plant. Swedish furniture is made in Poland, finished at home, then exported. Japanese and Hungarian interests are building plants in India.

Still another type of business arrangement has been created by US Hilton International and by US Intercontinental Hotels (a Pan American Airways subsidiary), which supply know-how, arrange financing and, in some cases manage hotels under various types of contract in Eastern Europe.

Smaller in scale but equally dramatic is the counter-thrust of Eastern combines in the West: the USSR's automobile assembly plant in Belgium, its oil refinery in Antwerp and in Brazil, participation in a steel complex in France; Poland's phosphate undertaking in Canada; Hungary's potash mine in Saskatchewan; Yugoslavia's pharmaceutical company in Switzerland; Romanian building contracters in Germany; the Comecon-Benelux Trucking Co.; Bulgaria's fifty-fifty trading partnership with Italy's Gaetara Zacca in Switzerland, etc. Joint ventures with Western firms to supply plants and technology in Turkey, Spain, Latin America and South East Asia are expanding.

Perhaps the most ideologically shattering trend of all is the communist movement towards capitalist banking. Soviet-owned banks like the Banque du Nord in France and the two successful Moscow banks, Narodny in London and Wozchod in Zurich, have operated profitably in the capitalist money market for a considerable length of time. The comrade managers enjoy a high reputation among the many banking potentates in London's City, Geneva's Place Bel Air, and the Place de la Bourse in Paris.

Yugoslavia's top bank, the newly-formed Beogradska Banka, of Belgrade—in terms of funds the biggest bank operating in Yugoslavia—intends to be active on the international money market through membership of the London-based International Investment Corporation for Yugoslavia, and also through consortia formed with banks in Bulgaria, Czechoslovakia and Hungary, according to a statement just issued in London. It will operate in London, Paris, Milan, Toronto and Tehran through representative offices and joint companies, and will correspond and maintain current accounts with nearly 400 banks and financial institutions. It has sixty-four offices and branches within Yugoslavia. Also in London are Czechoslovak, Hungarian and Bulgarian banks. Eastern European banks (Hungary, Poland and Bulgaria) operate in Austria, Beirut and Iran too.

Paralleling the surge to multinationals in industry, the banks are also joining new East-West consortia. A recent example is the 'Centropa' bank formed by banks of seven countries in January 1971 to 'promote technical co-operation, investment and trade between Eastern and Western countries'. The seven Centropa partners are Banco di Sicilia (Italy), Banco Popular Español (Spain), Bank of Tokyo (Japan), Banque Occidentale pour l'Industrie et le Commerce (France), Kleinwort Benson (England), Bank für Arbeit und Wirtschaft (Austria), and Bank Hadlowy W. Warszawie (Poland).

The London branch of the House of Rothschild announced that it had contracted to raise capital loans of several hundred million dollars in the West for various investment projects of the Romanian government.

Another interesting initiative is that Eurodollars are now going East. A banking syndicate led by the manufacturers Hanover Ltd and by the Moscow Narodny Bank of London have granted a $7·8 million medium-term Eurodollar loan to the Romanian Foreign Trade Bank to finance the purchase of aluminium-manufacturing technology from American

Metal Climax for an aluminium sheet-rolling plant (first stage capacity 21,000 tons p.a., second stage 113,000 tons). The term for different components of the load ranges from five to seven years, with a floating interest rate to be adjusted every six months at about 1·5% above the cost of funds to the banks. The banking syndicate includes the USSR-owned French Banque Commerciale pour l'Europe du Nord, Bank Winter, Banque Européene de Tokyo, Gebr. Roechling Bank, Girard Trust Bank, Ibero-Amerika Bank, Interbanca, Kleinwort Benson, Manufacturers Hanover Trust Co., and Ultrafin SA.

Undoubtedly, the most clamorous happening in communism's evolution to capitalist banking, and the most indigestible for the theoretical purists, is the establishment of a 'Comecon Investment Bank', which began operating in January 1971 with the declared intention of making profits. Set up by the Soviets, the bank includes all the Eastern states. According to Mr Vitaly Varobyov, its Chairman, the new institution will buy and sell currency, gold and securities, and will float interest-bearing bonds on international markets. One of the primary aims is to raise capital for promoting Eastern development, especially long-term credits of up to fifteen years, on Western capital markets. Given that it is ultimately a state-owned enterprise, the bank will be able to manipulate its interest rates arbitrarily, despite its assurance that it will be guided by capitalist–profit motives. The probable repercussions on the West's liquidity and interest rates is too obvious to need any comment.

EXPERT OPINION

David Rockefeller
Chairman of Chase Manhattan Bank

Speaking to a forum of businessmen in Rome in March 1971, David Rockefeller called for more US trade with the Soviet and Chinese Communist blocs to replace the iron curtain with 'a plate-glass curtain'.

The US banker conceded that 'helping the people of the Eastern European Communist bloc countries to enter the era of mass automobile ownership or selling them computers will not solve the major problems that divide East and West'.

But Mr Rockefeller noted that the United States had lagged far behind Europe and Japan in building commercial bridges to the Soviet bloc and mainland China. He welcomed the recent relaxation of some US restrictions on trade with Peking, and Washington's approval of the sale of computer components to Romania.

Mr Rockefeller noted that Hungary and Romania had made some progress in moving from bureaucratic, centrally-administered planning to greater autonomy for individual state enterprises and even some reliance on markets. Discussing Communist societies Mr Rockefeller said that 'a disenchantment with controlled government planning can be seen in countries like Poland and Yugoslavia'.

'I believe that the time is right for foreign investors with tact and empathy to accelerate the flow of private investment to countries indicating a desire for greater economic liberty and political freedom,' Mr Rockefeller said.

V. The Case Against Wages

FACT VERSUS FANTASY

Workers are losing the race against inflation. Real wages have been stagnant or rising very slowly in most countries. The US Department of Labor reports that since 1966 there has been almost no gain in the real wages of American workers. The average US weekly wage in 1957–9 was around $98·00. For the nine-year period since 1961 this has risen less than 11%, a little over 1% per year. At this rate, the mythical 'average worker' in the United States could expect to double his personal living standards once every century.

During 1969 and the first half of 1970, price increases accelerated in eleven out of seventeen OECD countries, at an annual rate of more than 5%. In Germany, Italy, Norway, and Sweden, the rate of increase more than doubled. But by the middle of the year the peak of the price rise was passed, and during the latter part of 1970 the seven major countries saw a significant slowdown in price increases to below 5%, and less than 2% in Canada and Germany.

In contrast to prices, wage rates increased considerably less in 1969 and the first half of 1970 than in the second half. Fourteen of the seventeen OECD countries recorded higher increases towards the end of 1970 than in 1969. These opposite trends buttress the argument that the larger increases won in 1970 and 1971 were, in the main, a recovery of real wages lost during the crest of the price wave in 1968, 1969 and early 1970.

French automobile prices, for instance, have considerably outstripped the rise in direct wage costs of the industry in the last three years. Since 1968 they have risen by around 30%. Nominal wage rates have risen about 35%, and real wages of French auto workers 18%. But given that unit wage costs constitute less than 25%, of the total retail price, it is evident that it is not wages which are the primary cause of the price rise, despite the claims of industry.

No wages explosion occurred in the years 1965 to 1968,

during which time increases averaged around 7% with the exception of Japan. The claim that the world-wide acceleration of price rises which occurred in 1968, 1969 and 1970, were due to rising wage costs during the previous years is therefore patently untenable.

If there was any correlation between wages and prices during the years up to 1970, it was a negative one, given that wages and prices moved in opposite directions. The relatively strong wage rises in late 1970 through 1971 are also entirely consistent with the argument that the larger increases in wage rates this year are the backlash of the price inflation of the last three years. Money wages can scarcely be indicted as the cause of inflation in face of these figures which clearly demonstrate that they are its victims.

The inflation effect of high marginal income-tax rates is seldom considered in indictments of rising rates. Following a period of stagnant real wages, such as occurred during the period between 1965 and 1969, the income-tax effect accentuates the range of wage rises needed for workers to recover lost ground, especially in high-tax countries such as North America, the British Isles and the Nordic countries. In formulating wage demands, unions are being forced to consider the pre-tax and post-tax value of the wage rise, which can be substantially different, especially for the higher wage groups who fall into the more steeply rising tax brackets. For example, in Great Britain, the average tax rate for workers is around 30%. This means that to raise real disposable income by 10% in order to make up for price rises, nominal pay increases would have to be 15%.

The 1970 wages explosion occasioned by the over 10% rise in rates (after direct and indirect taxes and price increases are accounted for), according to the *National Institute Economic Review* (March 1971), produced a situation in which consumers' real disposable income rose only by 1½%.

To compensate for losses in real wages due to a 4% rise in prices, during 1970, German workers in the $300-a-month wage group with no children must on average have an 11% nominal increase (between 9 and 17%). The comparatively steep tax progression and the increased deductions from salary for social insurance, mean that, to match the losses due to a 4% inflation, German workers need to raise their wages and salaries around triple the rate of inflation. According to leading labour economists, American workers will need a 9% pay rise just to keep ahead of a 5% inflation, and to keep up with average productivity. For incomes in the $7000 to $9000 a year range, a 9% increase would boost real income by only 5 to 6 %, as nearly a third would be taken by tax boosts. To achieve the 9% in real terms, the increase would have to be over 12 to 14 %.

A growing number of countries experienced rising unemployment in 1970. The annual 100-nation study of the ILO reports that the increase in the number of unemployed during the year was most marked in Canada, USA, France, Japan and Morroco. As of June, unemployment in the USA exceeded 5%. In Canada it rose to 7%. Particularly significant was the fall in employment in manufacturing in leading industrial countries like the USA, Canada, United Kingdom, Switzerland and France. In contradiction to the accepted postulates, prices did not fall in sympathy. The ILO reports that the rate of inflation rose in sixty-four countries with most registering a rate of increase of more than 5%, as measured by the cost of living. For the seventh consecutive year, Brazil, Chile, South Korea, South Vietnam and Uruguay led the trend with price increases of more than 10%. The United States, United Kingdom, Japan, France and Sweden were among the countries recording an increase of more than 5%.

THE ANOMALY OF HIGH AVERAGE/LOW UNIT WAGES COSTS

An article published in *Fortune* magazine in February 1971 succinctly illustrated the simplistic wage cost-push theory of inflation with customary 'this is it' finality. 'The global wage inflation', it oracled, 'was caused by union power, of monopoly abetting monopoly and redistributing income by force, breaking down time-tested wage differentials which must be restored at the cost of more inflation.' And this monopoly power, it implied, with corroborating photographs of leading international trade unionists, was being applied everywhere in every industry at the same time.

EXPERT OPINION

Newsweek, February 1, 1971

'On the face of it, [in the US] the factory workers' weekly wage jumped nearly 50% in the past decade. Even after discounting rising prices, real wages rose substantially until 1966. Since then, however, there has been almost no gain—a major cause of labour's militance at the bargaining table.'

Milton Friedman

Economist
University of Chicago

'Wage increases are the result of inflation, and not its cause.'

Wall Street Journal

'Labour costs aren't the Frankenstein monster they're cracked up to be.'

'Labour Costs, far from soaring, are only inching upwards nowadays. Some analysts, in fact, predict labour costs may soon begin to decline.' The *Journal* stated that widely-publicized reports of large hourly increases at the collective bargaining table, 'do not give a true picture of the trend of labour costs. They show only what has been happening to wage rates—and then only wage rates to unionized employees. It is a fact that pay to workers has been getting bigger but also that labour-cost increases have been getting smaller. . . . In the last few years, labour costs have been declining to a point that in the last [three] months, the Index has barely budged, rising a miniscule one-fifth of 1%.'

It was bound to happen. Unproven, gratuitous assertions that organized labour is overreaching itself have become the leading arguments of incomes-and-prices policy protagonists. The pivotal argument balances precariously on the charges that union power is driving money rates and, automatically, unit-labour costs out of sight, and that rises in the well-organized branches are transmitted eventually to the more marginal sectors which have to raise prices.

The latter ritualistic incantation can be disposed of summarily. In the differentiated, mixed economies of the West, holding money wages down to levels prevailing in the retrograde industries would result in inadequate effective demand and recessions. Only by exporting an exceptionally large part of GNP could any reasonable balance be maintained, and this is an increasingly difficult achievement in an era when capital and management, rather than goods, are the factors which increasingly move over borders.

The crisis in the UK, provoked by the misguided attempts by the goverment to pursue a conspiratorial incomes policy by forcing low wage settlements in the electrical power-supply industry and the post office on the basis of national productivity estimates and not on the industries themselves, is evidence of the prospective effects of such policies. This route leads inevitably to impasse and to conflict; it is unenforcable and inept, unless bourgeois politicians are ready to put workers in jail, with implications which will make inflation appear unimportant.

The wage-cost argument falls entirely apart when assessed against changes in unit labour costs over the last few years. OECD statistics on the movements of wages and salaries, unit labour costs and prices bring this out very clearly.

On the basis of 1966 = 100, the ratio of US prices to unit labour costs in 1970 was 93·3 in the third quarter. Unit labour costs were only 17% higher in 1970 than in 1966, even though wage rates were up 24%. In Canada, unit labour costs for the four-year period rose 16%, in Japan around 5%, France about 6%, Germany around 10%, Italy 16% and the UK 19%. These figures do not support the wage-cost inflation argument, which is based upon changes in nominal rates (see the Tables at the end of this chapter), unless, of course, one agrees with the article in *Fortune*, that 'the notion that labour has a right to share in an industry's exceptional profitability is dubious to begin with'.

But if this right is removed, what justification remains for a worker to agree to measures for improving productivity? The proffered rewards for abstinence through generally lower prices, more employment and the supposed benefits of capital expansion for all workers alike have always turned into mirages and disappeared when sought. In living memory they have not been received without struggle.

The theory that price stability necessitates maintenance of historical wage differentials between the low productivity branches with high unit labour costs, and the high productivity branches with low unit costs is both economically unsound and politically neurotic. After decades of strident proclamations that productivity must be the criterion of wage rates, it is ridiculous beyond reason.

Any politician or labour leader who seriously attempts to sell the idea that it is not the productivity or profits of the firm or industry in which he works that counts, but the state of the national economy, had better have alternative employment opportunities available. If corporate and industrial profits of the branch or company in which they work are no longer the legitimate concern of workers in regard to wages, but only those of the national economy, surely this eliminates any justification for maintaining the myth of the private market economy, and supports advocating a collective economic system on socialist or collective items, or at least bureaucratic state capitalism if guarantees of the interests of the incumbent elite are still desired. It is irrational to argue for enterprise-controlled profits in a private open economy and simultaneously press for a collective wages policy.

A dramatic example of the differentials between national averages and specific industries is the major household appliance industry of the US which makes kitchen ranges, refrigerators and washing machines. From 1959 to 1969 productivity in this branch rose nearly 90% compared with a rise of about 35% in the economy as a whole. Another example is the rise in the productivity of US agriculture, especially of foodstuffs. Because of technological advances in the land, one agricultural worker today supplies enough food for forty-six people compared with a 17–1 ratio two decades ago.

Equally significant is the pattern in which wage increases have occurred. Statistically, this knocks out another prop from under the wage-cost inflation theory. For this theory to hold, the rate of wage and salary increases must be proportionately higher in the weakest organized, low-productivity industries. Only then can price increases be attributed to rising unit labour costs.

In the capital-intensive sectors, high nominal wage rates are not correlated to costs in any meaningful way because of the high productivity and low unit labour costs which has improved over the decade faster than money wages.

A recent United Nations study on the *Economic Aspects of Automation* confirms the unit-labour-cost reduction effects of capital investment in these terms:

'If capital becomes cheaper and the quality of labour and capital remain unchanged unit costs drop. Then a large-scale enterprise will employ more capital and less labour for producing a given quantity of production. Automation only intensifies the cost-reducing effect of lower interest rates, by introducing even more of the cheaper capital.

'Substitution of labour by capital, whereby there is a quality increase in the factors of production, is much more frequent than automation without such a change. The part of the increase in overall productivity not due to changes in the factor prices derives from technological progress. It is quantified by the extent of the drop in unit costs at constant factor prices.

'Apart from these cases where automation is essential for technical or health reasons and for which no general conclusion can be made, automation always results in a drop in unit costs at constant factor prices. The presumably relatively infrequent cases in which the costs were wrongly evaluated are not considered. The decrease in unit costs may be due to reductions in labour, materials and energy required per unit and/or to advantages of mass production.

(a) *Reduction of unit costs*

'The reduction of unit costs as a result of automation may be due to various reasons: the plant size; decreased overhead costs; increased production rate; decreased needs for skilled labour or to a higher rate of capacity use.

'(1) A large enterprise produces a sufficiently large volume of products more cheaply than a small one. This is mainly due to the more efficient organization of production and management of large enterprises, their more favourable conditions for purchasing and financing, etc.

'(2) Overhead costs, calculated either once for the production run as a whole, or from time to time for fixed periods, will decrease per unit of output if the output increases.

'(3) Machines generally work faster than men; they produce a larger number of products in unit time. Therefore, fixed costs which depend on time can be spread over a large number of items in the case of a greater use of production capacity. The higher the production rate can be raised, the lower will be the unit costs at a given level of fixed costs.

'(4) In non-automated enterprises the skill and experience of the labour force increase with increasing output. The time required for each operation therefore gradually decreases. This possibility is removed as a result of automation. Machines do not possess the capacity of learning from experience. The personnel entrusted with the adjustment and servicing of machines do, however, have the possibility of forming routines. In spite of the fact that the costs and time required for starting automated production processes are often heavy, automated production processes yield savings because of a much lower need for skilled labour.

'(5) In so far as automation can increase the daily production time, it not only raises output per time unit but also the number of hours worked. Thus, the fixed costs can be spread over a larger output volume.

'An enterprise can reduce costs if it succeeds in raising its rate of capacity use as a result of automation.

(b) *Unit cost structure*

'Beyond a critical volume of output, unit costs are not only lower under automated production, but are also made up differently. Displacement of labour by capital tends to increase the proportion of capital costs in unit costs and leads to the decline of labour costs. The components of capital costs, interest on the capital invested and the amortization, also increase the size of fixed costs, as well as personnel costs, which are independent of output and dependent on time because of a rigid employment plan.

'It is therefore, important to separate costs into time-dependent and output-dependent (costs for materials, direct labour, fuels, etc.). Meeting costs in the case of an automated production process depends primarily on a high rate of capacity use.

'The extent to which the cost structures can vary for

TABLE V. 1. *Structure of the processing costs for a modern oxygen-steelmaking plant and a Thomas steelmaking plant (1965) (Shown in Percentage of Total Cost)*

Item	*Oxygen-steelmaking plant* (sub-items)	*Oxygen-steelmaking plant* (total)	*Thomas steelmaking plant* (sub-items)	*Thomas steelmaking plant* (total)
Labour costs*		17		25
Power costs		10		9
including gas	1		3	
electricity	8		5	
water	—		1	
other froms	1		0	
Capital costs		26		16
including depreciation	18		10	
interest	8		6	
Maintenance and repair		12		11
Plant and equipment		18		16
Fuels		4		7
Other costs		13		16
Total processing costs		100		100

* Including wages for repair and maintenance work.
Source: *Economic Aspects of Automation*, United Nations, 1971.

different automated production processes is demonstrated by comparing the structure of the processing costs in an oxygen-steelmaking plant and a Thomas steel plant, which were started at the same time in the same enterprise. Per converter and per ton of steel produced, the oxygen-steelmaking plant required one-third less production personnel (see Table V.1 p. 129).

'In the Thomas steel plant, personnel costs are highest, but in the oxygen-steelmaking plant first place is taken by capital costs. The power, maintenance and repair costs have also risen (see Table V.1).

'Although there is agreement in the literature that capital costs increase with technical progress, views differ on the progress of maintenance and repair costs. Because of the increase in technical efficiency, the costs for raw materials and semi-finished products tend to drop relatively. The interest changes on stocks of raw materials and finished products also drop relatively, since it is generally possible to reduce storage time by accelerating the flow of materials.

The Economic Commission of the EEC in a recent survey conducted into comparative national wage levels in fifty industrial branches found that wage rates differed much more from country to country than from industry to industry. This alone undercuts the wage-cost argument. In analysing changes in wage rates between April 1964 and April 1969 on a country basis, the commission found that

'. . . average hourly wages in manufacturing were 31% higher than the EEC average in Germany, and 7% higher in Belgium and the Netherlands. On the other hand, average hourly wages were 10% and 27% lower in France and Italy, respectively.

'At the EEC level, mid-1969 hourly wage rates in the petroleum industry were 47% higher than the EC average rate in manufacturing. Other above-average sectors were automotive (19%), aviation (18%), machine tools (11%), and chemicals (11%).

'Geographical factors seem to be less important than structural considerations. Wage rates in the same industrial sector of various countries are relatively more homogeneous than those of different sectors in any country. In each country, the ranking of industries according to wage costs is nearly identical.

'Between April 1964 and April 1969, average gross wages in the manufacturing sector rose 57% in the Netherlands, 47% in Belgium, and 39% in Germany. The five-year increase was 41% in Italy where, despite the heavy pressures of politically strong labour unions, wages still trail those of all other EEC countries.

'During the same period, the highest wage increases in the Netherlands were registered by the food industry (63%), followed by chemicals (62%), rubber (60%) and paper (60%). In Belgium hourly wages rose the most in the chemical sector (57%), followed by rubber (52%), petroleum (50%), electrical machinery (47%), and paper (47%). In Italy and Germany, sharp increases were registered in the petroleum, paper, and rubber industries, which showed wage hikes ranging between 39% and 43%.'

Strong unions are, of course, one aspect of the relatively high rates in the chemical process industries in all the countries. However, these levels also reflect the similarity of structural factors and the unmistakable feature that labour costs in these industries have become unimportant compared to capital plant and equipment, which makes enduring strikes a very uneconomical proposition for management. It is revealing that the higher stakes of earnings in the chemical, rubber, glass and petroleum industries were accompanied by a much lower number of strikes than in metal, motors construction, etc. So it is not the monopoly of union power which seems to apply in reality, since the incidence of trade union organization and power, measured by the proportion of workers organized and the strength of the different industrial unions, is generally stronger in the branches where wages rose less rapidly.

The recent United Nations ECE report on the European Economy in 1970, commenting upon wage and non-wage shares of value added per person in different-size enterprises, stated that

'differences in value added per person employed may be accounted for by differences in wage levels, or in gross profits, or in both.

'For very *broad* size groups, a close association appears to exist in a number of countries between size of establishments or enterprises, output per head, and investment per head. If output per person employed increases with size, at least up to a point, investment per person employed increases even further. In the United Kingdom, in 1963, the 98 biggest enterprises accounted for about 37% of total employment in manufacturing, 40% of output and 47% of investment. In Italy in 1965, enterprises with more than 500 employees accounted for 30% of total employees, 40% of value added and about 60% of fixed investments. A similar picture, but with steeper progression, emerges when *output*, rather than employment, is taken as the measure of size. For the Federal Republic of Germany, a few summary figures on output, fixed investment and employment, at different *output* size, are presented in Table V.2. The data (for 1963) refer to enterprises other than plants or establishments.

TABLE V. 2.

COMPARATIVE STATISTICS

Size class by turnover size (Million) DM)	*Employees per enterprise*	*Net output per employee*	*Investment per employee (Thousand DM)*	*Investment per unit of output (Thousand DM)*	*Wage and salary bill per employee*	*Share of wage and salary bill on net output (percentages*
2	47	16·0	1·8	0·112	6·4	39·9
5	95	16·8	1·8	0·109	6·7	40·0
10	200	17·4	1·9	0·108	7·0	40·3
25	405	18·5	2·1	0·110	7·4	40·2
50	893	18·8	2·3	0·123	7·6	40·3
100	1705	19·7	2·5	0·125	8·0	40·6
1000+*	7612	24·7	3·9	0·159	8·9	35·9

* Employment in this class accounts for 27% of total employment in manufacturing (Data refer to 1963.)

As can be seen from the figures for this one year, both output and investment per employee increase, and more investment is made per unit of output, as size of enterprise increases. The last column of the table shows, for the highest size group, a considerable drop of the wage share in net output. This is because output per employee rises more (54%) than the wage bill per employee (39%) when moving from

FIG. V. 1.

Index of Unit Wage or Labour Costs
manufacturing, in U.S. dollars
adjusted for seasonal variations
1966 = 100

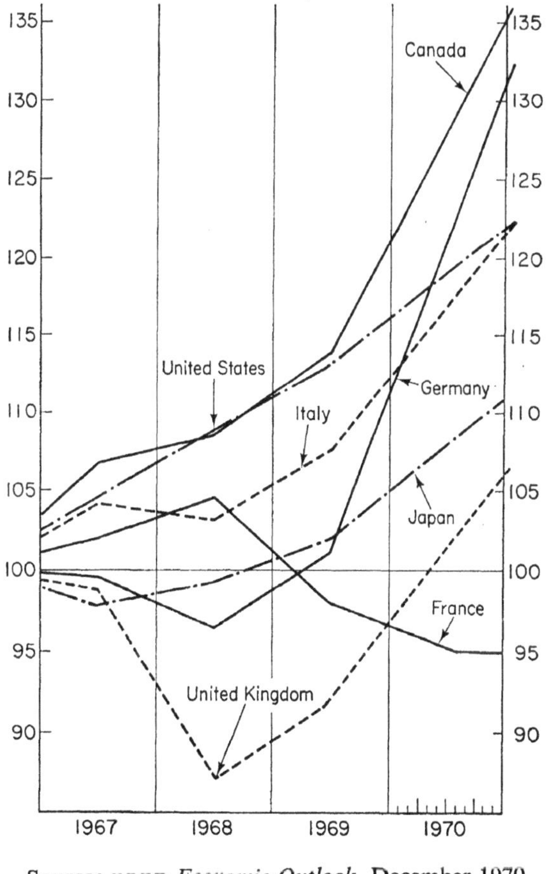

Source: OECD *Economic Outlook*, December 1970

the smallest to the highest size group. Thus, in the larger enterprises, capital costs take a bigger share than labour costs of total output than in the smaller (less capital-intensive) enterprises, even though the average wage level increases with size.

TABLE V. 3.

GERMANY
Index, 1966 = 100

	1967	1968	1969	1970 Q1	1970 Q2	1970 Q3
Industry (s.a.)*						
Wages and salaries per manhour	105·1	111·6	122·6	136·8	137·5	143·1
Production per manhour	105·4	115·3	123·5	125·8	128·2	127·1
Unit wage and salary costs	99·5	96·4	98·8	108·8	107·1	112·2
Prices						
Consumer prices	101·5	103·3	106·0	109·0	110·0	110·1
Industrial producer prices	99·1	93·9	95·9	100·4	100·9	101·7

* Excluding public utilities and building and civil engineering.

ITALY
Index, 1966 = 100

	1967	1968	1969	1970 Q1	1970 Q2	1970 Q3
Manufacturing						
Hourly wage rates	105·2	109·0	117·2	136·4	141·1	143·9
Number of wage earners	103·5	105·3	108·6	110·4	110·9	111·6
Production (s.a.)	108·4	115·2	118·8	128·0	125·6	..
Unit labour costs (s.a.)	104·1	103·1	107·5	114·1	116·0	..
Prices						
Consumer prices	103·2	104·6	107·3	110·7	112·2	112·8
Wholesale prices:						
Investment goods	100·0	101·3	108·0	118·9	120·5	120·5
Consumer goods	99·5	99·4	103·2	108·3	109·8	109·8

UNITED KINGDOM
Index, 1966 = 100

	1967	1968	1969	1970 Q1	1970 Q2	1970 Q3
Manufacturing (s.a.)						
Average earnings	103·3	112·0	121·1	129·1	132·4	135·7
Employment	97·2	96·4	97·4	97·2	96·7	95·8
Output	100·0	106·3	110·0	111·0	110·4	111·0
Unit wage and salary cost	100·4	101·6	107·2	113·0	116·0	117·1
Prices						
Consumer prices	102·5	107·3	113·2	116·9	119·7	121·1
Goods and services (excluding food)	102·5	107·5	113·1	116·6	119·0	120·9
Wholesale prices:						
Manufactured goods (excluding food)	100·8	104·7	108·0	112·3	115·2	117·0
Raw materials (excl. food)	98·4	109·3	113·5	117·9	117·2	115·1

Source: OECD *Economic Outlook*, December 1970.

UNITED STATES
Index, 1966 = 100

	1967	1968	1969	1970 Q1	1970 Q2	1970 Q3
Manufacturing (s.a.)						
Wages and salaries per employee	103·6	110·8	117·2	120·8	122·1	124·3
Output per employee	99·5	102·1	104·4	103·5	103·4	103·8
Unit labour costs	104·7	108·7	113·0	117·4	118·0	119·8
Ratio of prices to unit labour costs	96·5	95·3	94·8	93·7	93·9	93·3
Prices						
Consumer prices	102·8	107·2	112·9	117·2	119·0	120·3
Goods less food	102·5	106·3	110·8	113·1	114·8	115·7
Wholesale prices	100·2	102·7	106·7	109·8	110·3	111·0
Manufactured goods	101·2	104·2	107·9	111·3	111·2	111·9

CANADA
Index, 1966 = 100

	1967	1968	1969	1970 Q1	Q2	Q3
Manufacturing (s.a.)						
Wages and salaries	107·0	114·3	126·5	132·4	133·4	136·0
Output	100·3	105·4	111·3	112·2	111·4	109·4
Unit wages and salary costs	106·7	108·4	113·7	118·0	119·7	124·3
Prices						
Consumer prices	103·5	107·9	112·8	115·5	116·5	117·1
Wholesale prices	101·8	104·0	108·8	111·3	111·0	110·1
Manufactured goods	102·0	104·7	109·6	111·0	111·2	110·6

JAPAN
Index, 1966 = 100

	1967	1968	1969	1970 Q1	Q2	Q3
Manufacturing (s.a.)						
Monthly earnings per regular worker	113·2	130·1	151·4	161·7	173·2	185·2
Production per regular worker	115·8	131·2	148·4	160·8	168·1	170·8
Unit wage and salary costs	97·8	99·2	102·0	100·6	103·0	108·4
Prices						
Consumer prices	104·0	109·5	115·2	121·2	122·8	124·2
Wholesale prices	101·9	102·6	104·9	108·2	108·9	108·8
Producer goods	102·2	101·8	104·0	108·5	109·4	108·5
Investment goods	100·7	101·5	102·0	102·7	103·5	104·2

FRANCE
Index, 1966 = 100

	1967	1968	1969	1970 Q1	Q2	Q3
Manufacturing						
Hourly rates	106·0	119·1	132·6	138·8	143·1	146·3
Production (s.a.)	102·7	107·7	122·3	129·3	127·9	129·2
Unit wage costs (s.a.)	102·0	104·5	102·1	102·0	106·9	107·3
Prices						
Consumer prices	102·7	107·3	114·2	118·0	119·7	121·2
Wholesale prices	99·2	100·6	109·2	117·9	119·7	118·5
Intermediate goods	99·3	97·5	107·4	115·3	117·8	117·4

Source: OECD *Economic Outlook*, December 1970.

VI. The All-Consuming Search for Capital

THE ADDICTION TO ECONOMIC GROWTH

Corporate growth is like drug addiction: the stronger it gets, the greater the need and dependency. Both have exploded into social epidemics and seem in danger of getting out of control. Putting them back under control will, however, not be an easy task. Years of malignant neglect has produced an almost total inexperience in how to deal effectively with them. The obsessional search for larger and larger capital 'fixes' to feed its intoxicating growth needs has become the principal driving force of the economic organism. In a few years the incremental advantages of private capital investment will be exceeded by the incremental disadvantages in the degradation of the environment, technological unemployment, and economic crises. The net social effect of corporate investment will be negative. Like most hard addictions, this is a habit acquired in an effort to escape responsibilities and obligations particularly in regard to changing and reforming a meaningless uninspiring economic and social order.

Almost no concern is shown for the long-term secondary consequences which may arise. Yet it is the second degree, even third-degree, consequences which can be so costly and harmful. Efforts to apply technology are usually immediate and saleable and the advocate groups are well-organized and politically influential. No such organized force exists on the opposite side for the secondary effects are usually global and long-term, and most users, consumers and citizens are too taken up with the problems of earning a living and bringing up children, or fighting the desperate social scourge of old age, for involvement in counter-crusades.

EXPERT OPINION

Dr Harry Brooks

Dean, of the Faculty of Engineering and Applied Physics, Harvard University

'Unless we very soon develop better measures for technology assessment, it is likely that ill-considered political reaction against technical progress will produce a crisis in our society which will make the environmental crisis look tame by comparison. . . . Thus I regard technology assessment as essential to continued progress.'

Ralph Nader and 'consumerism' in the US, and the new citizens' political groups organizing outside parliaments and parties, may be the first stirrings of a response. These incipient protest movements reflect a growing uneasiness that investing in all sorts of technologies to provide, for instance, better mousetraps, gadgets and gimmicks, or to reduce flying time from Paris to New York to two hours only to spend hours waiting to land and fighting street traffic to one's destination, are largely counter-productive. Increasingly horrific accidents caused by cars built to go a hundred miles an hour on roads little better than macadamized wagon trails, and similar anti-social, anti-personal phenomena is not progress. The question now arises—does the advertising industry create and condition consumers to want new products of industry, or does industry change and produce useless products to keep the advertising industry prosperous? In the US more is spent on advertising than on education.

Using more technology to increase unemployment and turn out products which have not been analysed or assessed relative to their social utility does not herald a bright future. Blindly pumping more and more capital into meaningless enterprise in order to produce more toxic products, useless drugs and superfluous services with less workers is approaching the stage where man is in fact turning himself into a robot programmed for self-destruction.

His programming is especially deficient in the economic and political spheres. The complex, thousand-equation, econometric models are beginning, through a subtle combination of parental pride and insidious feed-back, to determine the type of questions being asked, finding the appropriate questions to fit the built-in answers. These models today are formulated and programmed to demonstrate how wage-costs produce inflation, rather than to analyse whether they do or not. Re-working these complex computer models from fundamentals could take years, and would certainly be subject to the laws of institutional inertia.

As a result, society is becoming crisis-prone. Change tends to be responsive only to crisis or to a high level of conflict and threat. Economic decisions, as they ascend from the enterprise board-room to government committees, become ever less effective. In direct relation to the levels at which they are taken, decisions become compromises, arrived at by consensus and taken only in the short run. Policy is less able to anticipate and to deal with future problems, but merely concerns itself with those past or passing. In such a context of crisis-response, it is almost impossible to replace dogma, even when its irrelevance is clearly evident. The intricate defence systems which groups and institutional interests have built up, to protect the saleability of their goods and services, rest upon the credibility of their particular brand of wisdom. Keynesian economists, Freudian psychologists, dialectical Stalinists or *laissez-faire* capitalists therefore do not surrender their bags of magic easily.

In time, of course, change does take place. Neither the capitalist system of today (which apologists like to term 'mixed economies' but which in fact are public-private configurations patterned in the interests of the private sector), nor the Soviet system of state capitalism (controlled by the military–party–management bureaucracies) are what they were a few decades ago. But in the policy areas, change occurs too slowly to be meaningful. Both systems suffer from chronic hardening of the arteries in all except the investment networks. Increasing investment in technology is the common overriding drive, though the means of control and distribution are held to be mutually antagonistic. But the cult of blind investment and the cult of technology are endemic to both.

THE CAPITAL GAP

The greatest capital gap in history is now opening up in the United States, a fountainhead whence flows much of the best and worst in the world. Increasingly, this gap will dominate economic decision-making and corporate strategy, and will exert a decisive influence over most other economic factors, notably prices.

During the period 1966 to 1970, the United States invested $235 billion in long-term capital, the highest figure on record. Authoritative estimates put the long-term capital needs for the five-year period 1971 to 1975 at $418 billion—an increase of $183 billion or 78 %. This means an average annual increase of nearly 16 %. A short fall of at least $100 billion is foreseen and it could go up to $120 billion in the economy as a whole. GNP reached $1 trillion in 1970, after 200 years. It is expected to reach the second trillion by 1990 (some forecasts say even by 1980).

For corporations alone, the 1971 to 1975 needs in long-term funds are projected at around $168 billion compared to $105 billion raised during 1966–70, an increase of $63 billion or 60 %. In the previous five years, American firms raised only $13 billion of their capital from the equity market, equal to only 12 % of the total. The rest came from debt financing and retained earnings. Although it is expected that corporations will increase their long-term equity capital to $33 billion during the next five years, this will still only represent a fraction of their needs.

A questionnaire on the 1971 investment plans of private industry of the European Economic Community, by the European Commission, revealed that, despite strong contraction tendencies in the economies, a sustained high level of capital investment was anticipated. In no case was there expectation of a reduction in absolute terms from the record levels of 1970, as in every country rises—from 5 % in Germany (over its 24 % rise in 1970) to 16 % in France are forecast. Even in Belgium where investment rose by 50 % in 1970 over 1969, a further rise is foreseen.

CASE CAMEOS

Herr Friedrich Thomee
Director of Finance and Executive Board Member of Volkswagen

Volkswagen would have to seek outside financing this year for the first time, Herr Thomee declared. This will be needed to meet future investment requirements, he said. Previously all Volkswagen investments were financed out of reserves. Despite the lightness of capital, he said, Volkswagen is not planning to make any cuts in future investment estimated to amount to about DM 4·5 billion (nearly $1 billion) over the next few years.

Rhône-Poulenc

President's letter to stockholders, 1970

France's largest company, with a turnover in 1970 of 11 billion francs, writes:

'. . . beyond short-term reactions of clients, it seems that large developments are forseeable in the markets interesting the group and in order to satisfy them an important programme of investments has been established for 1971, 1972 and 1973.

'This programme is of exceptional scope since it involves a total industrial investment of 5 billion francs. Our objective is to assure three-quarters of the financing of it through the revenues of our own group.'

In its economic survey of Europe in 1970, the European Economic Commission of the UN reported that fixed investment continued to support the expansion of output in 1970. In Sweden, and the United Kingdom there was little increase in investment in 1970. In most industrial countries, total fixed investment grew by 6–8% in 1970, markedly increasing its share of GNP. The increase was still greater (over 10%) in Austria, the Federal Republic of Germany and Finland.

The expansion of investment in 1970, as in 1969, was mostly concentrated on machinery and transport equipment (at least in the few countries for which information is available). This reflects the steadiness of industrial investment, which appears to have increased in most countries by 10–20% (except in Ireland, Sweden and the United Kingdom).

In France, the growth in fixed long-term investment has been spectacular during the past years, funded almost entirely out of internal corporate cash. But shortages of long-term capital are foreseen for the first time. Total investment is expected to rise from 182·2 billion francs ($36·5 billion) in 1970 to 344 billion francs ($68·6 billion) in 1975—an increase of nearly 90%. In real terms, this represents a rise of close to 73% at around 15% a year. Industrial investment is expected to rise from 125·2 billion francs ($25 billion) in 1970 to 241 billion francs ($48·2 billion) in 1975, which is 94% in monetary terms and 75% in real terms. It has been announced that this will necessitate finding 40 billion francs a year of long-term funds which the corporations will not be able to raise internally.

While Germany is expected to dampen the rate of capital growth in 1971, it will not be anywhere near predictions and will rise close to 5% over 1970, to around DM 180 billion ($47 billion). Public investments will continue higher at around 12% however. Only DM 20 billion ($5 billion) was raised on the public capital market in 1970 including both debt and equity financing. Italy on the other hand, is expecting a very strong rise in fixed capital investment of between 5% and 7% following increases of over 8% in 1969 and 1970.

EXPERT OPINION

Dr Hans Buchner
Managing Director of Osterreichische Stickstoffwerke AG (OSW)

Group turnover of Austria's largest chemical firm, OSW, rose by 10% in 1970, with sales of parent company up around 8%. Dr Buchner reported that one half of the 1971 investment programme of Sch. 350 million is destined for petrochemicals. The long-term investment plan of the parent company, covering ten years and an expenditure of some Sch. 8 billion, Dr Buchner stated, 'is faced with difficulties in that the present proportion of borrowed funds to internal funds was extremely critical'. He implied it would be impossible to increase the share of borrowed money further and requested the state to increase OSW capital, and/or provide help through higher prices.

M. Paul Huvelin
President of the French National Manufacturers Association (CNPF)

'More than ever the pursuit of expansion appears the major imperative of French society. Outside this road there is no hope of improving living standards, increasing the number and quality of jobs . . . development of collective equipment improving the environment. . . . But this expansion takes place by the development of the productive capacity of exports. French enterprises are affirming their dynamism: a recent survey indicates a growth of 20% in the number of investment projects compared to 1970. However, it is important that the lack of means does not compromise its achievement.'

Japan's rate of long-term investment is expected to decelerate somewhat in 1971, from the 18% capital growth of 1969 and 1970. But even this will only reduce capital growth to a rate of around 14%, still the highest of any country in the world. If the growth continues at even this level, Japan, today already third in the world capital league, will be the world's most capital-rich nation by the end of the century. Its people in contrast will probably still be modern feudal serfs, amongst the most consumer-poor. Japan's growth is based upon investment. It has had the highest fixed capital formation of any country—32% of GNP compared to 22% for West Germany, 21% in France, around 20% for Italy, 17% for the UK, and 17% for the US. It has also had the highest rates of inflation and the highest percentage increases in wages. This destroys the myth that growth, especially in a country poor in resources such as oil, coal, steel, etc., must give precedence to exports such as the UK and French officials are insisting upon. Japan exports only 10 to 12% of its total output, about half as much as the UK and France.

A number of countries are facing shortfalls in capital to fund their programmes. Even allowing for a certain easing in demand for long-term capital, the absolute volume of new funds in the world will be under tremendous pressure to satisfy business. There is talk of rationing Europe bond issues and Eurodollar borrowing to prevent runaway interest rates in the latter part of 1971 and in 1972. The rise in the index of planned or estimated long-term investment in almost every case exceeds other aggregates by a considerable margin: production, prices, wages, etc. There is convincing evidence at hand of a worsening climate for corporate financing. Both the cost of fixed-interest borrowing and the availability of bank credits will develop disadvantageously for investors. Recently a spokesman for the German industry warned that the traditional sources of self-financing and bank loans were no longer sufficient for industry's needs and that shareholders would have to make capital available to meet growth targets.

THOSE WHO HAVE SHALL RECEIVE

The entire problem is exacerbated by growing international competition for funds, especially to finance overseas expansion, and an inadequate, inequitable institutional system for raising and allocating capital. First the money market is highly concentrated and structured to make it largely a closed club for most borrowings. The largest banks and industrial corporations are highly integrated. In the US, commercial banks control over three-fifths of the total institutional investment of more than $1 billion in US industry. A recent survey pointed out that 49 large banks hold 5% or more common stock (usually enough to ensure control) in 147 of the 500 largest corporations. The significance of this is even more evident when the fact that only 200 corporations out of a total of 2000 possess 60% of American manufacturing assets.

The German magazine *Der Spiegel*, early this year in an article on the German Banking system, declared that private banks control and administer 70% of all the voting shares of German industry. The interlocking ownership in Italy between the large companies such as FIAT, Montedision, SNIA, ENI, IRI, etc., and the banks, makes it almost impossible to differentiate or distinguish between them in any meaningful way. The number of French companies controlled by or associated with 'Suez et Union parisienne' are legion. It is not without significance that the president of France's largest industrial enterprise, Rhône-Poulenc, is a former chairman of the Bank of France.

Japan's pre-war Zaibatsu have been almost completely reconstituted. The mammoth enterprises like Mitsui, Mitsubishi, Sumitomo, Kawasaki and others which conglomerate through all divisions of industry, commerce, finance, insurance and through steel, electronic, chemical, paper, and engineering production, all possess their own banking chains. The relationship between the Zaibatsu banks and the central bank (Bank of Japan) is exceptional. It is as if the private sector controlled the public sector. All the outside capital of Japanese firms (85%) is debt capital, the loans of which are guaranteed by the central bank. There is no need to seek equity capital or dilute ownership. All of the retained earnings and funds in the banking system are available for investment. About 100% of deposits of the Japanese banking system are out on loan. The industry can do this because even though wage rates have increased, the broad trend of annual return on investment is 33%, which is almost entirely re-cycled into further investment.

The result is that the international capital money market is very narrow for independents, and operates as a very strict rationing system. This is why changes in the interest rates, particularly prime rate adjustments, no longer influence the investment plans of big business nor effect the flow or volume of credit. Such modifications have become largely symbolic.

EXPERT OPINION

David Rockefeller
Chairman of New York Chase Manhatten Bank

'The global shortage of capital will require new and larger responses by international financial institutions.'

Andreas Whittam Smith
City Editor of The Guardian

'The four clearing banks made profits of just over £200 millions before tax in 1969. Their reserves add up to almost £428 millions.

'These figures were given in 1970 for the first time. Hitherto the banks have published results substantially understating their actual earnings and capital resources. In each bank, only a handful of top executives have known the full picture, and none has known how well or badly their rivals have been doing.

'It turns out that the clearing banks have been earning between 17 and 20% on capital employed which, by the current standards of British industry, is a handsome return. On the other hand, 1968 and 1969 have been exceptionally profitable years for the banks because of the high level of Bank Rate. Publication of the figures can be expected to have three main results. The banks themselves will now become a good deal more profit-conscious than they have been able to be in the past.'

BANKS CONTROL PRODUCTION

Central bank discount rate policy is thus another outmoded, only partially effective arm of increasingly impotent public policy. Large firms are guaranteed their supply of funds by their captive or patron banks. IBM generates so much money within its system around the world that it is its own banker. So are Michelin, ICI, RKZO, Fiat, Ford and Nestlé. The integrated capital supply system is under constant pressure to raise the real cost of money to provide a larger share for the services of the banking divisions. *Fortune* magazine wrote in 1967 that the hard financial core of capitalism in the free world is composed of not more than sixty firms, partnerships, and corporations, owned or controlled by some 1000 men. These men head investment-banking houses in New York City, merchant-banking ventures in London, *banques d'affaires* in Paris, and similar institutions in Belgium, the Netherlands, Italy, Germany, Sweden, and Australia. Among them they raise, directly and indirectly, an estimated 75% of the $40·6 billion in fresh capital needed each year to fuel the long-term growth of the industrialized nations.

In Paris, the important *banques d'affaires* include the Banque de Paris et des Pays-Bas, Crédit Lyonnais, Banque Worms, Banque Rothschild—and Lazard Frères. In London there are perhaps a dozen major merchant bankers, including such leading ones as N. M. Rothschild, Morgan Grenfell, S.G. Warburg—and Lazard Brothers. In New York, two dozen investment bankers dominate the world's largest capital market; they include Morgan Stanley, Lehman Brothers, First Boston Corp.—and Lazard Frères. All of these banks are extensively involved in various joint ventures with one another, forming one vast, closely interrelated power block.

Instead of raising more funds and contributing to greater liquidity, these institutions, by soaking up funds for the growing appetite of their capital-hungry clients, induce scarcities elsewhere and make it more difficult for the smaller firms to acquire long-term capital except at exceptionally high interest rates.

THE MONEY INDUSTRY HAD A GOOD YEAR

One of the consequences of this highly structured and integrated world capital market is that the product or commodity price of money is rising constantly. Reported profit figures by major banks for 1970 were unprecedented. In fact, it was a vintage year. The impressive thing is that it occurred in a climate of narrowing net profit margins, falling production and sales in industry, and strong inflation in the economy.

The Bank of America Corporation, the largest US Commercial bank, reported earnings around 11% higher in the fourth quarter of 1970 compared to the year earlier period. Assets rose from $25·57 billion to $29·74 billion.

The giant New York Chase Manhattan Corp., presided over by David Rockefeller, reported a fourth-quarter profit rise of 37·5%, bringing earnings gain for 1970 to 16%. Its assets jumped from $22·2 billion in 1969 to $24·5 billion in 1970. Chase's New York rival, the First National City Bank, reported assets in 1970 of $25·8 billion compared with $23·1 billion, a gain of 12%. Profits rose around 17%. Compagnie financier de Suez et de l'Union parisienne, the mammoth French investment firm in which the British government hold an interest of over 13%, reported net profits up 20% during fiscal year 1970. The company had 250 million francs in reserves, and an investment portfolio of over 500 million francs spread around the world. J. P. Morgan and Co., New York's fourth largest bank had a year round rise in profits of 24·2% in a net income of $86·6 million. Over the final period of 1970 net income rose by 28%.

Major Italian banks reported sharply higher profits for 1970. Banco di Roma's net income rose by 47% to 4·5 billion lire ($7·2 million) from 3·07 billion lire in 1969. Credito Italiano reported a 34% gain in net profits to 4·82 billion lire, as compared with 3·59 billion lire for 1969. French banks generally had an extraordinarily profitable year in 1970. Almost without exception their final statements showed over a 20% net rise in their consolidated positions. Banque Nationale de Paris declared a 21% rise in earnings, the French Société Général 25·4%, le Crédit Commercial de France around 22%. And this was after more liberal provisions for reserves and working capital than ever before.

The giant Société Générale de Belgique, financial holding company, the real ruler of the Belgian economy according to informed thinking, reported a sharp increase in net profit of nearly 13% to 714·4 million Belgian francs ($14·3 million). Real earnings or cash-flow not reported climbed well over 20%.

Switzerland's three biggest banks reported historic highs in growth of assets and good profits for 1970, with Union des Banques Suisses (UBS) showing a gain of 10·6%, Société de Banques Suisses (SBS) 11·2%, and Crédit Suisse (CS) 10·2%.

The Banque Européene de Crédit à Moyenne Terme (BEC) almost doubled earnings and more than trebled its balance sheet total in 1970, the third full year of operation. Created specifically to furnish medium-term credit finance by a consortium of Europe's biggest banking institutions, its business in 1970 included deals with 120 concerns in twenty-three countries. Profits rose to $2·08 million from $1·15 million, and the balance-sheet total increased to $495·3 million from $163·9 million.

But more illustrative of the banks' bonanza than their net profits is their growth of assets. Most of the banks have been increasing their assets at an enormous rate during the 'inflation years' as the table on the following page of the 'top twenty' European banks discloses.

Coming at a time of strong inflation, such growth in earnings and assets has provoked widespread comment, including charges of profiteering, discrimination in lending, and engendering an interest-inflation. Several sceptical critics of the banking system have even suggested that the reduction in the prime rates which spread around the world early in January of 1970 were carried out more to offset such criticism than in response to any significant improvement in liquidity and long-term funds in the private banking system. In any event, what is certain is that the highly criticized national and international systems which are supposed to mobilize long-term funds for capital investment which banks are required to provide out of short-term deposits, exercise a considerable influence on the real cost of capital. The net effect of this function is to further debilitate the influence of public policy on capital markets.

EXPERT OPINION

Philippe de Weck
Director General of Union des Banques Suisses (the Country's biggest bank)

'Other enterprises, called marginal, in economic jargon,

TABLE VI 1

European Banks

Rank '69	*Bank*	*Country*	*Assets ($000)*	*Increase over Previous Year %*	*Deposits ($000)*	*Loans ($000)*	*Branches and Agencies*
1	Barclays Bank	(Britain)	14,017,424	3·87b	12,507,675	9,995,800	5082
2	National Westminster Bank	(Britain)	10,641,566	8·01b	9,650,645	7,813,668	3915
3	Banca Nazionale del Lavoro	(Italy)	10,218,408	14·95	8,849,493	7,588,679	227
4	Banque Nationale de Paris	(France)	10,104,315	30·19	8,251,116	8,373,354	1719
5	Crédit Lyonnais	(France)	9,513,793	20·41	7,422,416	8,325,400	2022
6	Westdeutsche Landesbank Girozentrale	(Germany)	9,365,640	19·77	8,806,068	7,319,316	6
7	Deutsche Bank	(Germany)	8,685,905	17·21	7,590,106	5,864,741	1043
8	Banco Commerciale Italian	(Italy)	8,135,627	9·74	7,229,875	4,728,099	518
9	Midland Bank	(Britain)	7,796,275	2·15b	7,136,784	5,576,957	3521
10	Société Générale	(France)	7,768,838	11·16	6,586,732	6,468,783	1682
11	Lloyds Bank	(Britain)	6,691,574	4·13b	5,977,822	4,585,169	2533
12	Dresdner Bank	(Germany)	6,633,854	14·62	5,830,615	4,171,940	800
13	Banco di Roma	(Italy)	6,434,915	29·32	5,781,165	3,684,950	275
14	Credito Italiano	(Italy)	6,155,050	19·89	5,429,704	3,343,882	299
15	Standard & Chartered Banking Group	(Britain)	5,680,566	10·34	5,340,322	2,772,640	1365
16	Union Bank of Switzerland	(Switzerland)	5,584,297	32·23	5,078,633	3,885,078	137
17	Commerzbank	(Germany)	5,205,900	14·10	4,686,784	3,744,286	743
18	Swiss Bank Corp.	(Switzerland)	5,050,438	30·84	4,595,264	2,899,217	103
19	Swiss Credit Bank	(Switzerland)	4,777,007	34·25	4,337,149	3,429,251	75
20	Algemene Bank Bederland	(Netherlands)	4,390,928	30·23	4,145,566	3,290,461	585

because their margins [profits] are very minimal or non-existent, will not be able to absorb these increases. If, because of competition, they are unable to increase their prices, there will be no other solution for them but liquidation or, probably more frequently, to save what can be saved, merger with a stronger enterprise. . . . In matters of finance, tendencies can change much more rapidly than economic affairs. What one can say without risk of error is that capital [in 1971] will remain scarce.' Because of salary hikes, inflation credit restrictions and public budgets, he says, 'the [Swiss] demand for capital will be very high from this side. The capital market will thus remain under pressure and it is probable that all the needs will not be satisfied.'

Despite the vigorous rate at which central banks have created new credit, the switch from modest economic growth designed to provide full employment in the fifties and early sixties to the needs of fuelling breakneck expansion in capital spending, in consumer expenditure, in armaments, in construction, etc., dried up untapped sources of savings. By the end of the decade the needs exceeded the means of the central authorities to create new money without stocking inflation. The demand for capital outstripped supply and chased interest rates through the roof. This gap in capital supply and demand will become greater in the 1970s and make capital the most sought after and consequently scarcest factor of the economy.

VII. Cash-Flo-Flation

PRODUCTION IS A FACTOR OF CAPITAL

The large corporations today seek to optimize their profitability, not their profits. It is not just a difference in terminology, but in the basic motivation of business. This stems from the change in the ownership of industry and the uncoupling of management from stockholders. Entrepreneurs or stockholders traditionally have sought to accumulate private wealth or property, which implies taking profits out of the business for personal use and possession. With the gradual disappearance of the owner, most large undertakings are now controlled by fiduciaries such as commercial banks, investment trusts, insurance companies, holding companies, and the like. For these bodies the objective of profit accumulation is not important. Instead their interest and the aim of their professional management become maximizing the profitability of the enterprise in terms of how efficiently capital is used and increases itself. This transforms capital from a *means* for maximizing production to the *end goal* of corporate policy. The relationship between capital and production is thereby inverted: instead of capital being a factor of production, production has become a factor of capital.

The last ten years have fundamentally altered the classical parameters of the function of top management. The success of a company's development measured by discounted cash-flow techniques is the ratio of its cash flow to total revenue. Cash flow is the ratio which measures the proportion of gross income available for reinvesting after all external payments are deducted: wages, taxes, dividends, etc. Cash flow therefore gives an exact measure of the self-financing capacity of a company. According to this system, even dividends paid out to so-called owners is a cost and a drain on the company's 'profitability', i.e. the ratio of retained net profits plus depreciation to income. Thus, cash flow is the essential factor in assessing the state of the company and the success of managerial policy.

Cash flow provides two important data: (1) it reveals the true earnings and the financial and treasury situation of a company in a more realistic way than the very partial and limited figure of net profit; (2) it permits a more accurate estimate of the self-financing capacities of companies and the relationship of capital to wage costs, whatever the complexities of their self-financing policies. The ratios of cash-flow/turnover, cash-flow/net-worth or cash-flow/wage-costs are consequently much better criteria for measuring the annual and longer-term results of a company than the conventional net profits, return on sales, employee *per capita* productivity, etc.

Therefore net profits before or after taxes, prices of stocks compared with discounted earnings (P/E ratios), and other standards of assessing the results of a private business are no longer conclusive. The net profit figure, or distribution of net profits as dividends, is largely for outsiders and speculators. The objective of internal management is to maximize the return on invested capital. For example, SNIA Viscosa of Italy reported breaking even in 1970—no losses or earnings—in net profits. As a result it decided to forego paying a dividend to stockholders. But it announced that its exceptionally high rate of depreciation, about 15·5 billion lire, would be maintained, as would its very high investment programme which totalled 35 billion lire in 1970, the largest portion of which represents retained earnings.

This situation is typical in varying degrees of the modern corporation's policy of maximizing profitability. The successful US firms have been operating at around a 20% return on invested capital. In the high-capital process sector, it is up to around 25% after start up of full operations. French, German and Japanese giants are all well over the 20% and some over the 25% level. At this level, capital inputs would be returned in three to five years with the rest of the life-span of the capital goods producing pure cash flow. By comparison net profits are minimal and derisively low. In fact they have become a sort of ritual of the capitalist ideology, empty of significance, but symbolic of ancestry. Here are some examples:

TABLE VII. 1. *Some Revealing Net Profit–Cash Flow Comparisons (in millions)*

Company	*Currency*	*Turnover*	*Net Profit*	*Cash Flow*
Petrofina (1969)	Belgian francs	52,682	2,870	6,526
W. R. Grace (1970)	$	1,819	30,000	111,200
Bayer A.G. (1970)	D-marks	6,213	296	1,683
E. I. Du Pont de Nemours (1970)	$	3,618	329	1,000
SNIA Viscosa (1970)	Lire	340,000	0	50,000
Fiat (1970)	$	2,720	8,600	
ICI (1970)	£	1,462	89	343
Montedison (1969)	Lire	1,552,000	41,000	900,000
Hoechst (1970)	D-marks	3,013	316	2,490
BASF (1970)	D-marks	2,874	268	1,070
Royal Dutch/Shell (1970)	$	6,520	366	1,025
Alcan (1970)	$	1,389	80	230
SKF (1970)	Swedish Kr.	5,000	674	700
Siemens (1970)	D-marks	12,600	213	1,063
Michelin (1969)	$	1,000	85	200
AKZO (1970)	Florins	7,200	250	791
BSN (1970)	French francs	1,429	37	622
BP (1970)	£	2,659	91	247
Alusuisse (1970)	Swiss francs	2,302	129	308
Olivetti (1970)	Lire	465,000	6,440	22,000
Compagnie Française de Raffinage (1970)	French francs	3,681	87	442

Modern trends are intensifying this evolution. One such trend is the change-over from money and profits incentives to status power drives after a certain level of corporate size is achieved. Members of the 'billion dollar club', of enterprises having over a billion dollars a year turnover, obviously are involved in a power game rather than in getting richer. The top 500 corporations in the US have over $500 billion in sales. There are 65 European industrial firms and nearly 100 banking and commercial establishments which are members of the 'club'. GM does business of 24 billion dollars a year. It invests over a billion dollars annually. How except in terms of power-drives and motives of self-aggrandisement can its avarice for profits be explained?—particularly since most of its major stockholders are millionaires in their own right or are very large multimillion dollar institutions. Why should Rhône-Poulenc, FIAT, Shell and Wellenberg thirst for more money and self-righteously reject wage demands as something they cannot afford? The name of the game is 'growth', and the power this gives extends to the corporate technocrats and politocrats whose own influence and power are drawn from the process. Both the power plants and the grids which supply the energy and muscle for such growth are fuelled by capital piled up out of retained earnings. There is no alternative to this power struggle if the enterprise wishes to be among the two to three hundred leaders of the future.

Actually nearly 95% of investment in the Western world derives from cash flow. Certain industries, particularly the modern growth ones such as petroleum, chemicals, electronics, etc., have grown into giants on their diets of cash flow.

CASE CAMEOS

James M. Roche
President of General Motors
28 December 1970

Against a background of a 23% fall in sales for 1970 and a fall in 'profits' of 64%, James Roche, President of GM announced '. . . total capital expenditure in 1971 of about \$1·1 billion will be made to make the most of enlarged market opportunities in North America and overseas, and to meet rising environmental standards'. GM expects to spend nearly \$160 million in 1971 'on the control of air pollution from our products and plants', up about 7% from 1970.

Informed sources report that GM is working on expansion in Europe that may involve up to \$800 million spent over three years on up to five plants. Capital expenditure in 1970 was over the \$1 billion spent in 1969. 'The rise to \$1·1 billion', Mr. Roche said, 'was because our overseas commitments were somewhat higher than anticiapted. These overseas capital expenditures accounted for 20 to 25% of the total and will account for that amount in 1971.'

Leopold Pirelli
Chairman of Pirelli Rubber Co., Milan

In an interview recently published, Mr Leopoldo Pirelli stated that the cash flow of the company was around $40 million. 'One must consider that several subsidiaries (consociate) retain in their own operations a good portion of the cash flow which does not return to the parent; thus the figure of $40 million is under the true figure: for the foreign subsidiaries which belong to Pirelli International, we have a policy which is not immediate profitability. We cannot present a brilliant balance-sheet at present because we are pursuing a policy of expansion and above all expansion through self-financing.'

The Commission on Industrial Policy of the EEC estimates the proportion of self-financing of gross capital formation out of retained earnings to be approximately 100% in the US, UK, and Holland; 70 to 80% in Germany, France and Belgium; and 60 to 70% in Italy and Japan. When the specific industries and largest corporations are examined these proportions are even higher. Some major French industries approach 100%, and include motors, engineering, chemicals, glass, and electrical construction. In the VIth economic plan for the period 1971 to 1975, the Commission forecasts a still higher rate of growth annually—7·3% is projected as against 6·8% in the previous plan. Of this figure, 77 to 80% of total private investment is to be provided through self-financing. Sweden's auto, paper and chemical industries finance their growth entirely from profits. Seldom do Italian firms seek outside capital for their investments. External sources of capital have never been major considerations in Europe, where (with perhaps the single exception of the UK) the capital markets are extremely thin. But even in the UK, three-quarters of total British domestic investment is provided out of cash flow. Dividends paid out in 1969 represented only 15% of trading profits. It is noteworthy that, in spite of a stagnant economic situation, inflation and the highest average wage increases on record (about 14% according to government estimates), gross fixed capital formation keeps on rising. For the third quarter of 1970, it was $259 million higher at $2·3 billion, or 12% better than the previous quarter. For 1970 as a whole, not including the high volume of overseas capital transfers, the rise will be well over 10%.

Canadian capital spending is, as in most developed economies, highly concentrated in a minority of large firms. Inflation grew until the latter part of 1970, despite serious stagnation and unemployment reaching a level of 7% nation-wide. In critical areas like the Province of Quebec it is exceeding the level of 10%. But capital spending has continued high. In 1970, total capital outlays reached just under $6 billion. Despite the unemployment, it is expected to increase by 9%. Thus, the dilemma that investment and allowances are not sopping up unemployment, which stubbornly resists the macroscopic remedies. The most important part of the funds were out of internal cash flows.

With few exceptions, the key to the success of the modern corporations has been efficient cash-flow management. Not only has cash flow become the motor of their expansion and profitability, it has also been the channel to further inproving profit margins—contradictory though the thought of profits producing profits may appear at first glance.

To a very large extent cash flow modernists share the outlook that improvements in profitability are largely achieved by reducing the labour content of products. In the past, manufacturers, particularly in process industries and in durable goods, have been successful in automating away much of their labour force. The decade ahead promises to see a much further extension of the trend, even into the non-manufacturing branches. It thus is a self-generating process; increasing capital investment to automate labour out of the process and to reduce labour costs to enhance cash flow for greater capital spending, to automate further, and so on.

EXPERT OPINION

John Barber
Director of Finance and Planning, of British Leyland Motors

'At the moment we are not just earning *enough* to ensure we will be competitive in the future . . . and in the end that would mean contraction and in the end death.'

'British Leyland must grow bigger because its competitors are expanding all the time. . . . Our job is to maintain our position among the big boys. We are in the top ten.

'Profits in the first half of 1970 were only £1 million; the only other cash coming in was £40 million from depreciation.'

But British Leyland was investing at the rate of £50 million to £60 million a year in new Plant and tooling. So the 'money coming in does not cover the capital expenditure and the corporation is having to borrow more' to keep up with the spending of Continental motor firms which were investing between £80 million and £100 million a year.

M. Marcel Demorque,
President of the Groupe Lefarge (French cement giant)

'The group Lefarge has, as is known, an adjustable five-year plan for its investments, of great flexibility . . .

'For the period of 1961 to 1975 this plan foresees industrial and financial investments valued actually at some 860 million francs, or 170 to 180 million francs a year.

'Taking into account the necessary increases in working capital and repayments of loans, the global volume of investment for this period will reach 1·1 billion francs. The plan obeys two principles: assemble funds only in needed periods and make no appeal to stockholders.

'In this regard its own resources which will feed the plan will represent an autofinancing of 72 to 74% of investments.'

There is scarcely an important enterprise which is not

primarily concerned with improving its cash-flow function: Ford, GM, Du Pont, Standard Oil, International Paper in the US; ICI, Shell BP, BMC, the National Coal Board, Bowater and Reed Paper Companies in the UK; Siemens, Bayer, BASF, Volkswagen, and Krupp in Germany; Renault, Rhône-Poulenc, Michelin, St Gobain in France; FIAT, Pirelli, Montedison, ENI in Italy; Nestlé, Ciba-Geigy, Hoffmann-La-Roche, Brown-Boveri in Switzerland; Solvay, Petrofina, Unilever, Philips, RKZO in Belgium and Holland; and VOLVO, SKF, Billireud, Norsk Hydro, Borregaard in the Scandinavian countries, are only a handful of cash-flow oriented firms. Without exception, they practice cash-flow maximization and finance their worldwide expansion out of retained earnings.

A breakdown of British capital financing between 1964 and 1969 is particularly revealing:

TABLE VII. 2. *Sources of Capital Funds in UK Industry (£ millions)*

	1964	1965	1966	1967	1968	1969
Depreciation and retained profit	3,012	3,045	2,671	2,626	2,959	2,950
Investment grants	—	—	—	198	414	556
New issues in UK	412	408	575	415	482	512
Bank lending	696	474	231	269	517	615
Other	194	247	158	148	161	209
TOTAL	4,314	4,174	3,635	3,656	4,533	4,842

Source: Financial Statistics.

From these statistics it is evident that cash flow constitutes the primary source of investment capital in British industry. If investment grants, which were largely eliminated in 1970, and other sources, which are invariably hidden cash-flow reserves or internal capital of one kind or another, are excluded, the cash-flow source represents over 70% of primary capital inputs.

CASH FLOWS TO INFLATION

Because the modern corporation is a dynamic, vital organism, it projects and plans for the future. Profits are for ploughing back into expansion, not to be wasted on dividend pay-outs, which are kept just high enough to support stock prices and credit ratings. This turns the key management function around and permanently modifies the terms of reference in regard to wage costs and prices. Improving net profit margins or price-earning ratios of company stock is (according to capitalist folklore) management's prime obligation to stockholders. But in practice, cash flow gets taken care of first in cutting up the money cake and is the primary optimizing function of modern management. Net earnings are what is left over. That is why all the cost factors of production are adjusted to the imperatives of cash flow upon which the worldwide investment and marketing strategies depend. When turnover falls off, instead of prices being cut to bolster sales and restore income, as the textbooks propound, the loss in income is compensated through upward price adjustments at the lower volume. This is feasible because of the general price inelasticity of most consumer products and the administered price systems pervasive throughout industry. In the US, the least cartelized and presumably the most open-market economy in the world, 80% of consumer prices are administered by agreements—overt or convert. In Europe the myth of price competition is not taken seriously by anyone—not even by Ministers of Finance when they pay lip service to it in political sermons. Maximizing cash flow helps to explain the 'stag-flation' or recession-in-inflation syndrome, as it is the underlying cause of most of the price inflation being generated today.

EXPERT OPINION

Mr David Montagu
Chairman of Samuel Montagu and Company (important British Merchant Bank)
March 1971.

'The basic problem affecting the British economy is, in my opinion, the low level of investment.

'An awful lot of nonsense has been talked about the need

to increase investment without distinguishing the differences between good and bad investment.

'One of the strongest arguments for supporting the present Government's economic strategy is that if there was to be a freeze on incomes and prices at the current level of industrial profits, this freeze would have a disastrous affect on investment.'

He claims that UK industrial profits were too low to sustain healthy growth, and that investment since the war had been too slow, and, in many cases, extremely ill-judged.

'It is therefore completely right to embark on a long-term policy, as this government has done, which will result in allowing prices to rise, thereby increasing the profitability of the private sector while slowly clawing back the level of wage inflation over a period of time. This will help to create the sort of cash flow which is required to enable industry to embark on long-range investment planning of a type which will re-introduce into the economy genuine growth.'

Antoine Riboud
Director General of French Boussois, Souchon Neuvesel (BSN)

In a letter to BSN stockholders, Mr Riboud stated that 'for fiscal year 1970 the provisional net consolidated cash flow of the Group (SEB excluded) will be in the order of 313 million francs compared to 205 million in 1969', a rise of 52%. Net profit, while significantly greater is not expected to attain the 1969 level, however. 'This results essentially from the considerable increase in amortization . . . further, the importance of investments effected in the glass branches, contributes also to the increase in the volume of amortization for fiscal 1970.'

'BSN is thus pursuing its traditional financial policy of self-financing which permits it to limit the financial costs and to better profit from fiscal legislation, while maintaining a policy of rising dividends.'

For example, price cuts burden company policies and sales without providing correspondingly greater revenues. To sustain a given level of gross profits after a 10% price cut it is estimated a company would have to achieve 50% more sales, which is manifestly improbable, and the company would be forced to handle two-thirds more merchandise. Even assuming that a price cut increased a company's share of the market, it would not be likely to make up for the loss in income.

Cash-flow maximizing produces the same reciprocal price effect in regard to tighter liquidity, credit and high interest rates: the shortage of credit and augmented costs get reflected in higher prices rather than in cutbacks in capital spending. As interest rates rise and external credit lines dry up, companies are compelled to seek greater internal liquidity by upping prices. The terminal effects of deflationary fiscal and monetary policy at a certain stage thus become self-negating and the reverse of what is sought. Instead of a fall in demand with sales damping prices and lowering the rate of capital spending, prices rise to sustain investment. All higher short-term material and labour costs in cash-flow management are carried over into prices, in order to protect long-term capital needs. True, this reduces net profits below the line, but this is no longer a significant figure in modern large-scale enterprises. More significant is the above-the-line cash-flow figure which is the corporation's life-line to the future.

An American survey in 1970 came up with the finding that US business intended to increase its annual capital spending at a rate which would raise the total from $82·3 billion in 1970 to over $89 billion by 1973—double the yearly investments made a decade ago. This helps confirm the obvious fact, still incomprehensible to conventional wisdom, that capital investment is no longer responsive to the short-run changes in the economic climate. Contrary to the tenets of economic theory, modest declines in sales do not lever sharp mark-downs of investment plans. Nor do higher interest rates and government taxes seriously discourage them. Long-term prospects of markets and sales give fuel to capital spending plans today and dominate other factors of production. The long-run strategies of corporate planning puts an escalating platform under prices to provide the retained earnings or cash flow needed, regardless of vicissitudes in demand, government policies and economic theories.

SALES DOWN—SPENDING UP

In 1970 the American motor industry had its poorest sales year in over two decades: the annual rate of US-made cars fell from 7·7 million in 1969 to 5·5 million. It was over 10 million in 1966. In the UK, too, sales have been sluggish and the industry's output was down to comparatively low levels. Japan and Italy did not come up with particularly brilliant years in 1970 either. Nevertheless, all countries announced that their automotive capital investment programmes were being increased in 1971 and would rise steadily through 1975. Despite the ten-week strike, poor sales and a 65% fall in net earnings, GM forecast a rise in capital spending to a record figure of $1·1 billion, of which 25% was earmarked for overseas expenditure. Ford's 1971 investment was forecast at a record net $700 million—representing a 22% rise over 1970. Forty per cent of this is similarly for foreign spending. Neither GM nor Ford plan to tap their stockholders or their captive banks for their long-term money; it will be obtained through price adjustments. The British Confederation of Industry as well as the German Employers' Association have warned their governments of threats of imminent bankruptcies among smaller firms unable to get enough capital, unless they increase their prices and profit margins. They claim that the cause is wages, but it is readily shown that it is a shortage of cash which even a reduction in rates of wage increases would not resolve. The giant French rubber complex, Michelin, is reported to be investing new money at the rate of 4 billion francs ($800 million) in a five-year capital programme beyond depreciation inputs, in order to double capacity, further its research, and expand overseas. A $100 million investment in Canada to erect two factories (one for steel cord, one for radial tyres) is claimed to be the largest single European investment in North America.

EXPERT OPINION

Lee A. Ioccoca
Ford President
November 1970

Despite a mediocre sales year in 1970 and a drastic drop in net income of 5·6%, Ford's new President, Mr Lee Ioccoca announced 'investment plans for 1971 of $700 million, the highest on record, and over $130 million above 1970— Forty% ($280 million) is earmarked for foreign investment.' None of the funds will originate outside the firm.

C. B. McCoy
President of Du Pont de Nemours

In a year's-end statement Mr C. B. McCoy reported that profits in 1970 were 9% under 1969. Sales in 1970 remained substantially the same as for the previous year, around $3·7 billion. Despite this decline in profits and stagnation in sales, he announced that 'capital equipment expenditure in 1971 will increase at least to $500 millions compared to $480 million this year'.

That modern investment-oriented economies are inexorably moving to generalized and permanent inflation at rates of plateaux higher than the 2% to 3% 'compatible' figure of the past, seems to have begun to penetrate official thinking in 1971. The Canadian government, which achieved a comparatively low rate of inflation during the latter half of 1970, but which is still combating inflation psychosis, announced its intention to reflate the economy because of unemployment (which stood at over 7% in the first quarter of 1971).

The US administration, despite a 5% inflation, and in an

attempt to reverse the business downturn in preparation for the 1972 elections, announced cuts in 1971 business taxes of around \$2·6 billion. These allowances liberalized rules covering depreciation write-offs by shortening the time permitted for writing off machinery and equipment by 20%, and made the allowances more favourable for tax purposes. The Swedish government's 1971 budget provided similar tax benefits for capital investment through liberalized depreciation allowances in order to stimulate growth. Liberalized credit and borrowing conditions for industrial investment have been announced by both the French and Italian authorities. These changes in the direction of fiscal policy are being made despite an inflation rate of around 5%. It is a case of reflation upon inflation. It suggests that, as a matter of practical politics, certain governments are moving towards a policy of facilitating the building up of corporate cash flow. It is quite likely a pragmatic step in the proper direction, in contrast to a recent proposal of the Dutch government for a six months' statutory curb on wage increases over 5%. Augmenting the liquidity and cash flow of industry through such fiscal measures will stimulate investment without necessarily building pressures under prices. Of course, if it results in spending plans being raised even more, as is most likely, prices will continue rising. However, these proposals to ease tax depreciation rules on new equipment purchases will not significantly change capital spending plans in the short run.

One major US chemical company, summing up the chemical industry's attitude towards the proposed changes, said they will result in a significant cash benefit for the company over the next two or three years, but they will not cause it to alter its 1971 expenditure plans. As cash flow increases owing to relaxation of the regulations, however, the company adds, this could inspire a boost in equipment spending later on.

For many chemical companies, however, it will mean little, if any, change. For instance, Reichhold Chemicals' President, Stefan Baum, stated that his company, now in the middle of a major $50 million investment programme which was started in mid-1969, did not 'retrench when the liquidity crisis hit the US last year.' So, he says, in a sense, an easing in the depreciation rules would not help the company at this time or have much effect on its capital expenditure plans.

Another industrial spokesman reflected the general attitude of industry by saying that the proposed new depreciation schedule will have an immediate cash benefit in the form of working capital.

But others point out that the change in depreciation rules means that firms will really have to repay those cash benefits in income taxes in four or five years. Therefore, while the policy is in the right direction for them, it is not going very far or very fast.

CASH FLOWS IN THE 1980s

Shifts in the relative importance of industrial sectors and their repercussions on the patterns of investment have become key elements of the new cash-flow-flation. Extrapolation from 1969–70 trends points to a tripling of capital investment during the next decade in the big three sectors of the future: oil, chemicals and plastics. An authoritative Swiss economic research organization associated with the University of Basle has predicted that by 1985 the combined output of petroleum, chemicals and plastics industries will amount to around one-third of total West European production. The chemical industry alone will furnish a fourth. The study projects the doubling, even quadrupling, at running prices of Western Europe's total output to a value of around $1·8 trillion dollars. France's planning experts in their formulation of the VIth national plan projected that, by the year 2000, the chemical industry will cover the needs of 80% of French manufacturing. Given the greater weight of oil, chemicals and plastics in the total output of North America and Japan, their contribution to total world production will certainly be higher than 33%.

As the value of such investment (due to higher spending on technology, modernization, etc.) will stay ahead of output, the percentage of capital investment concentrated in these three industries will progress towards 38 to 40% of the world's total.

Currently, they account for less than 15 to 20% of total industrial investment. In 1967, for the seventeen industrialized member states of OECD, the percentage of chemical spending in the total of each country's manufacturing investment ranged from a high of 18·5% in Belgium and Holland to a low of 5·7 and 6·1% in Finland and Sweden respectively. By 1985 these rates will triple to between 30 and 50%. The mounting investment over the entire range of chemical-processing industries (which includes rubber, glass, pulp and paper, etc., as well as chemicals and plastics) will push the actual figure towards the 50% level. The jump from roughly a fifth to around a half of total fixed capital invested in manufacturing in just fifteen years represents a quantum jump to a new orbit of capital spending. When the electronic, transportation and electrical utilities and industries are added to the three petrochemical linked sectors, the total accounts for nearly three-quarters of all fixed capital investment projected for 1985.

The reduction of investment in the traditional sectors, in real terms, will occur at a far slower, more mechanical pace. There will not be a rush of old capital out of these into the new growth industries. Rather, it will recede gradually through attrition and non-growth. With only a limited amount of new funds and credit available from an inefficient banking system, the propensity to generate greater retained earnings through higher prices and labour displacement will necessarily intensify.

VIII. The Chemical Industry's Permanent Revolution

Capital investment in the US chemical industry in 1970 was greater than ever before. Inflation, slowdown of industry, fiscal and monetary restraints, the elimination of the 7% tax credit for investment had no effect. Domestic capital outlays were around \$3·4 to \$3·5 billion—a rise of 11% as compared to an estimated \$3 billion in 1969. Research and development budgets increased by over 10%. These statistics were estimated on the plans of twenty-four major US chemical companies, which account for over 85% of overall sales of basic chemicals.

And the US chemical industry will spend a record \$3·62 billion in 1971, according to the latest survey by the Commerce Department and the Securities and Exchange Commission. This would be 5% more than its capital investment in 1970. and represents a sharp upward revision from the 6% decline predicted in February. The survey also projects that chemical industry sales will be up 7·6% this year, compared to a gain of 1·9% in 1970.

INVESTMENT PLANNING IS LONG-TERM

The chemical industry is in a state of permanent revolution of technological change and expanding markets. The anticipated growth in chemicals in the Western world will more than double in the decade ahead, from around \$145 billion in 1970 to about \$338 billion in 1980. Predictions are for a \$400 billion market by 1985. World chemical investment will treble from \$12 billion in 1970 to \$34 billion in 1980, and quadruple by 1985. A rule of thumb used in the industry provides that for every dollar invested there is one dollar annual return on sales during the life on the investment. Even to keep their share of the markets, firms must maintain their capital expansion. Capital spending therefore cannot be turned off and on easily. The long lead time necessary for designing and funding chemical spending programmes make short-run adjustments difficult; indeed, in the larger firms they make it quite impossible. The same is true for research and development, which is the mainspring of chemical industry growth. Up to 20% of gross sales in pharmaceuticals are spent on research and this will rise to 30% by 1980. For chemicals as a whole it is close to 5% of sales and is expected to rise to 10% by 1980. The visible effect of such R & D on sales is more striking in regard to pharmaceuticals than in perhaps any other industry. The part of pharmaceutical production in the total sales of the chemical industry rose from 8·2% to 12% during the period 1950 to 1970. In the future, sales of pharmaceutical products will rise from around $18 billion in 1970 to $40 billion in 1980. By then the march of R & D expenditure will have topped $10 billion. This level of commitment further uncouples industrial investment from transient short-term cyclical shifts in the consumer economy. For most modern chemical firms, 30% to 50% of sales today are of products which were laboratory ideas five to ten years ago. In the US alone, more than 500 totally new chemicals are introduced commercially each year. This trend will strengthen and an even higher percentage of annual sales in the decade ahead will come from products fresh out of the research laboratories.

Huge losses also become a factor of capital costs at these rarified levels of R & D, as testified by the examples of the $100 million loss of Corfam to Du Pont, and the multi million dollar losses of many firms who overestimated the market conditions for certain types of artificial fibres during 1960–65. Even if a large part of such loss is recovered through tax reductions, the need for access to large amounts of money is still intensified. Dow Chemicals' $50 million write-off of German Phrix Werke, a joint venture with BASF, is another example. Unexpectedly huge costs in developing new materials for the R.B. 211 engine (for the ill-fated Lockheed jumbo), especially carbon fibres, contributed to the crashing bankruptcy of Rolls Royce.

Recent soundings of large US chemical firms point to a 2% rise in 1971 capital spending on plant and equipment over the record 1970 outlay of $3·4 billion. The largest companies are planning to maintain their outlays despite tight money and higher construction costs and despite a particularly poor net profit year in 1970. Union Carbide, Monsanto and Dow Chemicals report that they will hold their capital spending at near 1970's peak levels of $375, $300 and $325 millions respectively. Du Pont will spend more than $500 million, compared to $480 in 1970. Internal capital spending in 1970 was 14% higher than in the previous year. At the same time, and along with the first downturn in GNP since 1966 (during which US chemical investment rose about 9% annually), prices are expected to harden, which theory says does not happen.

Capital expenditure consequently has assumed a long-term orientation independent of net profits and annual fluctuations in sales and production. Over the past decade the annual growth rate of US capital investment in chemicals has been larger than the other indices of shipments, production and net profits.

Europe's chemical firms, with the exception of French ones, reported that 1970 was not a banner year for net profits. In the first nine months they dropped around 8%. Certain firms, like ICI in the UK, and Bayer in Germany, claim hefty wage increases to be the principal cause of their

TABLE VIII. 1 *US Chemical Industry*

Measure	1960	1965	1970*	*Percentage increase* 1970 *over* 1960	*Average growth raet per year*†
Shipments (billions of dollars	$26·6	$37·5	$50·2	88·7%	6·6%
Production index (1957–9 = 100)	116·6	173·4	243·8	109·1	7·7
Net income (billions of dollars)	$2·0	$3·2	$3·5	75·0	5·8
Capital expenditures (billions of dollars)	$1·55	$2·73	$3·46	132·2	8·4

* Preliminary figures or estimates. † Compounded annually.
Sources: Department of Commerce; Federal Reserve Board; Federal Trade Commission-Securities and Exchange Commission.

loss of profits. Shell Chemical claims wage costs rose some 12%, whilst Bayer alleges 20%. But chemical sales rose everywhere in Europe. 12% in Holland, 10% in Belgium, 10% in France, 8% in Germany. Interestingly enough only German firms, suffering a bit of indigestion, are slowing down investment programmes. But Bayer, which plans to spend \$1·4 billion during 1970–4, actually raised its planned target. BASF, which is also launched upon a \$1·5 billion spending programme, announced a cut back of 25% in 1970. However, 1971 spending is up at \$450 million. But in order to maintain their future markets, the German big three will go ahead with their announced plans to invest \$3 billion each during 1971 to 1975.

The French chemical industry's 1970 capital investment was a record \$2 billion, which was only 60% of the German chemical industry's capital spending of nearly \$3 billion, and 70% of the UK chemical industry's capital output of around \$2·5 billion. The latter UK figure was up 25% over 1969, and substantially in excess of the industry's previous peak year of 1966. All the others in 1971 will continue spending at higher rates than in 1970 and are all indicating that they

TABLE VIII. 2 *Growth rates between 1967 and 1970*

	1967 \$m	1970* \$m	*Increase* %
Du Pont	3102	3610	16
ICI	2349	3400	47
Union Carbide	2546	2020	18
Montedison	2092	2630	26
Hoechst	1671	2882	72
BASF	1276	2804	120
Bayer	1604	2600	62
Rhône-Poulenc	1116†	2020	81
Monsanto	1632	1971	20
AKZO	1194	1935	62
Dow	1383	1910	38
Ciba-Geigy	1096	1673	53
Cyanamid	937	1180	26
Sumitomo‡	306	554	81

* Company sources and CA estimates
† Figure is for 1966
‡ Year ends March 31

expect prices for their products to rise faster in the next couple of years than in the recent past.

Chemical firms have almost without exception outrun inflation. In spite of rising wage costs, their growth rates largely out-performed the average rate of inflation by a wide margin. A review of growth rates of sales in 1970 compared to 1967, published in *Chemical Age*, a British trade journal for the chemical industry, gave the results shown in Table VIII. 2 (p. 171).

EXPERT OPINION

Mr G. J. Wilkins

President of Beecham Group Pharmaceutical Division, and President of the Association of British Pharmaceutical Industry

The National Health Service of the UK, not wage costs, was responsible for the price of drugs in many parts of the world. Quoting record exports and omitting to report record profits, Mr Wilkins stated that

'other countries are unwilling to pay more for British drugs, the world's largest exporter, than prices the NHS fixes at home.

'It is becoming more difficult and expensive to launch new or improved drugs. The Swiss drug industry has shown that, where only five to ten years ago one newly discovered compound in 3000 reached the market, today it is only one in 5000. What costs the money nowadays is not so much the discovery of new compounds but proving that they are safe, effective and better than earlier discoveries.

'It is going to be increasingly difficult for new companies to break into the pharmaceutical market . . . they are going to need a very deep pocket indeed. A company must expect to spend at the very least £300,000 to £500,000 a year on research and development.'

Mr Pierre Baumgartner

Head of Rhône-Poulenc

An obligatory bond issue of 450 million francs was announced to stockholders, to help finance the enormous investment programme. This raises 6 billion francs ($1·1 billion) in three years including 436 million francs which will be allotted to research. Despite its importance, the triennial investment programme will be 75% covered by self-financing.

The chemical industry has traditionally relied upon retained earnings for its capital. German, French, British, Belgian and Dutch firms have generated their expansion funds almost entirely out of their cash flows. It is perhaps the industry in which the system of discounted cash flow is the most widely practised for determining the viability of specific investments. The total volume of cash flow in the American chemical process industry in 1969 was around $5 billion. Its composition was as follows: depreciation and depletion—$2 billion; retained earnings—$2·6 billion; increase in debt—$0·4 billion. For the European firms the increase in debt would be so much lower as to be negligible, for it is known that US enterprises carry a higher amount of debt to sales than is the practice in Europe, where almost total self-financing is the rule.

Cash-flow consideration will consequently push prices up by at least 10% during the year, adding a neat windfall to retained earnings of around 6% to 7% of sales, for even a 15% rise in wages should not result in more than a 2% to 3% increase in prices in order to recover costs. As usual, these increases will be put through amid a global cry—in Europe as in the US—that it is cost inflation and wages costs in particular which are responsible.

SOME FORECASTS OF FUTURE CAPITAL SPENDING

The Netherlands government planning-office forecasts growth in basic chemicals by 100% over the five-year period 1968–73, which implies an average yearly growth of about 15%. The realization of this production forecast will involve an investment of Fl. 7000 million.

The UK chemical industry, it has been forecast, will attain

a turnover of £10,000 million in 1985. Capital spending rose from £235 million in 1968 to £260 million in 1969, to £330 million in 1970. Over the next thirty years, it is believed that capital expenditures will possibly top £20 billion, excluding investment of oil companies in the UK (which is currently around £100 million per annum). Over the next three years, the National Economic Development Office (NEDO) forecast an average investment of £340 millions ($840 million) annually, compared to 1969 when the industry invested £265 million ($615 million). This represents a 28% increase. When the total capital spending of the oil industry, for example, is also taken into consideration, investment will be a spectacular £470 million in 1971 and £480 million in 1972.

The output of the German chemical industry will rise by between 7% and 9% per annum throughout the seventies, according to the most moderate estimates. In 1968 and 1969 the rate of sales growth was around 12%. In 1970 it was around 17%. This would lead to the anticipated attainment of a DM 100 billion ($44 billion) turnover by 1980. In view of the call for large-scale investments, the four leading firms would account for an increased share of the total. This figure also supposes a substantially higher rate of investment than the 10% turnover of the past five years, presumably about 14% to 15%, despite the predicted fall in 1971 of about 5%. In 1969, investment amounted to DM 6·5 billion, which was DM 2 billion or 45% over that of 1968. DM 1·5 billion of 1969 investment went into foreign operations and is expected to rise proportionately more than total investment in the future.

EXPERT OPINION

Professor Kurt Hansen
President of the German Chemical Industry Association

'Even evaluing the rate of expansion of the German chemical industry prudently at 7%, its production will double between 1970 and 1980. Its annual turnover will attain about 100 billion marks [$25 billion]. Investments increasing in proportion to turnover [the present rate exceeds 10%] it will become impossible to find the necessary capital on the German capital market. Recourse to foreign capital is bound to provoke the appearance of foreign subsidiaries, which will not be entirely under German control.'

A recent industry study on the future expansion of some Swedish chemical process industries up to the year 2000, envisages an expansion from the 1970 rate of Kr. 5 billion (about $1 billion) to Kr. 40–45 billion ($8–9 billion) calculated in fixed prices. This will be equivalent to an annual real growth rate of over 7% over the next thirty years.

The Italian State Holding company, ENI, has submitted a programme for the 1970s to the government which foresees tripling chemical output. Exclusive of synthetic fibres and artificial rubbers, the plan projects a rise from 3·5 trillion lire to 11 trillion (about $175 billion) in 1980. This represents an average annual increase of 10%. To achieve this goal, according to ENI's estimates, over 6·7 trillion lire ($10 billion—double the present figure) will have to be invested. This will be 14% of all Italian investment. According to the top industry association, total investment between 1970 and 1973 will attain 13·600 billion lire, or an average annual rate of 3400 billion. Compared to 2664 billion lire invested in 1969, this is an annual increase of 28%.

Japan's chemical industry spent nearly $2 billion in fiscal 1970 (ending 31 March 1971) for plants and equipment, according to a survey by the government's Economic Planning Agency. The study indicates that Japanese chemical firms having capitalization of at least $277,700 invested $1·78 billion for plants and equipment in fiscal 1970, while smaller producers (capitalized from $27,700) have allocated $161 million. The total—$1·94 billion—is an 18·9% increase over the previous year and is higher than the average for all Japanese industries, which rose 16·5% over 1969, to about $21·9 billion.

Forecasts are for a tripling of this amount to around $9 billion annually by 1980.

CHEMICALS HAVE BECOME A CASH-FLOW INDUSTRY

The importance of cash flow in facilitating such a scale of investment is evident from the above data. For example, the rate of growth of chemicals in the member countries of OECD, excluding synthetic fibres, was around 10% in 1970, considerably higher than for industrial production as a whole. The forecasts indicate a continued high rate of such expansion. This appears even more enormous when the oil industry is included, since this invests twice as much as chemicals and synthetic fibres, though the latter will rise at a faster rate. According to OECD statistics, world investment in chemicals (fibres and communist countries excluded) is running at over $8 billion a year at present. This will rise to around $10 billion in three or four years. This amount greatly exceeds the ability of capital markets to furnish. It is difficult to obtain accurate statistics on the volume of outside funds flowing to industry as a whole. One informed guess by the finance director of a major chemical firm puts the total worldwide flow of external non-debt funds to manufacturing firms annually at around $6 to 7 billion. As the chemical industry alone cannot hope to receive even 25% of this total amount, the uncovered portion will be enormous.

The only source of investment funds of such magnitude will be through bank credits, debt financing and cash flow. But bank credit will also be under strong pressure of demand from other industries, and is certain to be in critically short supply throughout the 1970s, regardless of the monetary policies pursued by central banking systems.

When these factors are taken into account, it is clear that the achievement of the chemical industry's ambitious investment programme will largely depend upon self-financing. For the chemical industry, maximizing cash flow has become the critical goal of dynamic management. The relative success or failure of cash flow management will largely determine the success or failure of the company in the seventies, and prices will have to keep rising to supply the capital.

'Price increases over a wide range of chemical products are seen as inevitable if the UK industry is to generate the cash flow needed to cope with a rate of expansion that is modest in comparison with all other industrialized countries.' That view was forcibly put by Mr Neill Iliff, President of the Chemical Industries Association, at the annual CIA dinner in London recently.

'The situation now is that the petrochemicals industry has a very small return on capital, and an inadequate cash flow to expand at the necessary rate,' he said.

EXPERT OPINION
Walter S. Fedar

Technomic Publishing Co., Technomic Publishing Computer Forecasts, USA

'US chemical capital spending next year (1970) will run between \$3·2 and 3·6 billion, with the lower level the more likely. By 1980, spending will pass \$7 billion annually. These outlays also mean more depreciation and resultant higher cash flow (net income plus depreciation). Cash flow could reach \$15 billion in a decade, about twice the present level.

'Expansions require more than internal funds, thus increased cash flow won't be all that's needed. The forecasted meteoric rise in capital spending will intensify need for borrowed capital. Long-term debt, which is nearing \$9 billion this year, will increase to between \$22 and \$25 billion in the next 10 years. Seemingly a staggering sum, this only amounts to a debt ratio of 27% compared with 24% now. The ratio is about the same; only the numbers are larger.'

Dr Rolf Sommet

President of Farbwerke Hoechst

Presenting the press with the first consolidated financial statement in the company's history, Dr Sommet, President of the Board of Directors of Hoechst, Germany's second largest chemical firm, stated that costs have risen as never before: 'Wage and salary costs rose 30·8% [this includes management, sales, etc.], or DM 460 million ($110 million), compared to 1969' but he admitted that 'the capacity of production and sales of the company grew considerably during the period. . . . The increase in turnover amounted to DM 840 million ($210 million) for 1970. Most significant was his elaboration that 'during the period, company and participating investment reached about DM 1·8 billion ($450 million)'. Depreciation attained DM 690 million ($150 million). 'Total investment of the group in 1971 will attain DM 1·3 billion ($325 million) without it being necessary to seek increases in outside capital.'

THE MERGER REACTION

The industry is also among the top three or four relative to the rate of concentration and integration generally. In fact small-scale, second-rank enterprises are being merged or bought out of existence as the industry follows in the foot-steps of petroleum refining's twelve-firm-industry.

Germany's rate of fusion is perhaps the most impressive, as it harks back to the time when IG Farben ruled supreme before World War II. Today, three offshoots of IG Farben—Bayer, BASF and Hoechst, which have over thirty-five joint ventures with each other—are rapidly reconcentrating into a *de facto* re-grouping of the Farben chemical empire. Over the last few years, BASF has absorbed such firms as Glasurit, Beck, Phrix, Herbol, Nordmark and Wintershall. Dozens more are on its list of probable takeovers. Hoechst has taken up Swarzkopf and Cassella; Bayer has grabbed Collopor and an important holding in Chemie-Verwalting.

In France the rush towards concentration has become frantic. Long controlled by banks and financial institutions, the holding companies are spreading their umbrellas and bringing in everything standing alone in the rain. Rhône-Poulenc first took over Progil, then Pechiney-St Gobain, and is now looking covetously at Ugine-Kuhlman. This leaves three groups in the country (including the public chemical sector), which will become only two when, as is inevitable, Ugine-Kuhlman succumbs. The steady process of merger in Holland, which has resulted in over a hundred chemical firms disappearing, is reaching a climax following the merger of AKU and KZO to form AKZO in 1969, the country's fourth largest combine.

The Italian process is equally predictable. Edison's take-over of Montecatini in 1966 to form Montedison is to end in its total absorption by the state-owned petroleum complex of ENI. This will leave only SNIA Viscosa outside this power group with a short life expectancy of independence.

Switzerland's Ciba-Geigy merger makes this group the sixth largest chemical firm in the world. The other large chemical enterprise, Sandoz, absorbed the three firms of Warder, Durand and Huguenin in swift succession. As it already has extensive ties with Ciba-Geigy through joint ventures, common sales outlets, and the like, the prospects for an eventual one-combine operation for most of Switzerland's chemical industry must be considered good.

More than any other factor, it is the need for capital and the size of worldwide operations which have been impelling the process of concentration. During the past decade, and certainly during most of the next, the pressing need for amassing, allocating and utilizing capital is and will be the motivating force behind the restructuring of the chemical industry's permanent revolution. The benefits of monopoly market positions, economies of scale, and very high value-added ratios are positive spin-offs, which churn in the wake of capital investment but are not its propellants. And the necessary multinational dimensions of capital spending on such a scale has made the global market the only one in which the chemical firm can live and prosper. National and regional markets would turn such groups into dinosaurs too large and massive to adapt to the environment and would condemn them to extinction. The scales have been reversed. Chemical firms don't grow merely to rule and control limited dominions; they must follow the lines of the force of technology and expand into capital-fuelled global orbits.

The alternative is a slowing down of their propulsion with the risk of falling back into their local habitat to be preyed upon and eventually devoured by the foreign multinationals invading their own back yards.

IN THE VANGUARD OF FOREIGN SPENDING

The chemical industry has long been in the vanguard of multinational investment. American chemical investment abroad is already running around \$1·6 billion annually. In 1971, this figure is expected to exceed \$2 billion—more than either the German and French chemical industries will invest in their own countries. The percentage rise in 1970 over that of 1969 was around 28%; it will be nearly 30% for 1971 over 1970. The book value of American direct foreign investment in chemical plant and equipment is around \$10 billion.

Most US chemical companies cite their foreign operations as the major area of growth during the past few years. These foreign operations have enabled some concerns to show year-to-year profit increases instead of losses. Hence, companies have earmarked a growing percentage of their overall spending for foreign operations. In 1971, for example, Dow budgets for 50% of its spending on new plant and equipment to go into overseas projects. Biggest of these is a complex based on a chlorine and caustic soda plant at Stade, West Germany, and second, a naphtha cracker at Terneuzen in the Netherlands. During the 1966–71 period, Dow will have spent \$592 million on overseas projects. Total operating investment by Du Pont's subsidiaries and affiliates outside the US was about \$1·3 billion in 1970; that is a rise of 10% from 1969. About 15% of overall spending will go into foreign projects in 1971. The largest foreign project is a \$25 million plant for Delrin acetal resins at Dordrecht in the Netherlands. About one-third of Monsanto's 1971 spending is for overseas projects. Two major ones are the 110 million lbs/year ABS plant at Antwerp and the maleic anhydride expansion (to 27,000 tons/year) at Newport,

England. Union Carbide plans to spend about $100 million (roughly 25%) of its 1971 budget on foreign projects. During the period 1966–71 more than $500 million went abroad. At home and abroad, therefore, leading US chemical producers are boosting their spending on new plant and equipment and on research and development. While they are still uncertain about the 1971 predicted business upturn, their 1971 investment plans show nothing but continued confidence in their industry's long-term future.

European chemical firms in 1968 had some $2·5 billion invested in the United States, which provided a sales volume of $5 billion. An authority in the US has estimated that extrapolating from the past rate of increase this could reach $10 billion with sales of $30 billion in 1980. Much of the massive investment of Germany's big three (BASF, Hoechst and Bayer) will go overseas, with a special priority allocation for the United States. Around 50% of their total turnover is already through foreign sales. BASF aims at 70% to 80% of its US sales being manufactured directly through subsidiaries in the country. ICI Europe will get more investment money than ICI in the UK. It already has over twenty-four plants spread around the Continent, operating under holding company headquarters ICI-Europe in Brussels.

The European chemical enterprises generally have an

TABLE VIII. 3

	Total sales in 1969 *$ millions*	*Overseas sales as proportion of total percentage*
Ciba-Geigy (S)	1,443	98*
Akzo (H)	1,759	84
Bayer (G)	2,415	64
Hoechst (G)	2,439	54
ICI (UK)	3,252	52
BASF (G)	2,427	49
Rhône-Poulenc (Fr.)	1,835	47
Dow Chemical (US)	1,797	36
Union Carbide (US)	2,933	26
Monsanto (US)	1,939	23
Cyanamid (US)	1,087	19†
Celanese (US)	1,037	17
Du Pont (US)	3,632	15

impressively higher proportion of total sales overseas than US firms, thereby confirming their basic multinational character. This is, of course, obligatory for big-league enterprises situated or originating in relatively small national markets. The two leaders as given in the table on p. 181 are (not surprisingly) the Swiss firm Ciba-Geigy, the world's thirteenth largest chemical firm, and the Dutch giant Akzo, the world's eighth largest.

The beginnings of an important American and European wave of chemical investment in South East Asia, Japan, Korea, Hong Kong, etc., has started, along with the reciprocal movement of Japanese firms to Europe—both directly and through joint ventures. The pace of foreign investments of American chemical firms in Europe grew ten times, from $44 million to $427 million. In 1970, this figure reached nearly $1 billion—or twenty-three times greater. The share of chemical investment to total US investment in the Common Market rose from 12% in 1960 to nearly 45% in 1970, making it the principal attraction (along with the motor industry) for investment. The relative share of foreign investment in the total spending of European chemical companies is growing even faster. Their investment and turnover will grow faster abroad than at home, especially as the late drive of the German (like the Japanese) chemical firms get under way. In just three years, European foreign direct investment in the US went up by a third from $9 billion to $12 billion.

Compared with the rest of industry, Japan's chemical industry, which mushroomed into a $10 billion giant in the 1960s, is also the leader in foreign direct investment. Estimates place Japan's overseas chemical investments at about $3 billion, and its expected rate of growth at about 50% annually during the next five years up to a total of $22–$25 billion on present trends. Most such investments are concentrated in South East Asia. But the US, Europe and Eastern Europe figure prominently in their plans. Mitsui Chemicals has set up a joint venture with Hercules in the US to produce high-density polyethylene and polypropylene. In addition to the new chemical complex in Belgium, Japanese firms have acquired production facilities in Brazil (Teijin chemicals), Venezuela (Kurashiki Rayon), New Zealand (Sumitomo chemical), Canada (Mitsubishi Shoji), France (Dainippon), Italy (Mitsui), and elsewhere. Such a movement, radiating out from an economy where low wages are supposed to be an irresistable source of attraction for American and European firms, helps demonstrate that past notions of corporate motivating and concepts relative to national economics no longer hold up. Low wages alone are no longer the exclusive inducement to overseas chemical investments, in fact not even the primary ones. The complexity of chemical corporations' global plans are enormous. They seldom conform to preconceived standards of economic behaviour. When Indian and Japanese firms begin investing in direct production in such high-wage countries as the United States, Canada, Switzerland and Belgium—dramatic examples which will be commonplace statistics in a few years—it is evident that something profoundly new is happening. Like inflation, wages are no longer the determining factor in investment. Thus, it is a global flow, with the major task of management being the filling of their world-girdling capital pipe-lines with basic material-money. As for industry generally this now includes the new sector of investment in the fifty-fifty partnership deals with Eastern European communist governments' chemical combines. The trend, as could be expected, is perhaps strongest in chemicals and is expanding faster than in other industries. In these deals, most of the fixed capital and equipment is supplied by the Western partner. The chemical firm of the 1970s will therefore no longer be a single national organization with foreign markets, but will be a multinational entity in its technology, products, markets, organization and financing. This will be true of American, European, Japanese and eventually Soviet firms alike.

WHATEVER HAPPENED TO LABOUR COSTS?

Chemical growth has exceeded national economic growth in

all countries, and is often almost double the rate. The differential will grow throughout the 1970s. Annual net investment for eight European countries nearly tripled in the decade from 1958 to 1967. In Japan, it was five times higher. In the US, with its already large-scale operations, the chemical industry more than doubled its capital input. The average annual increase was over 10% in Europe, 12% in the US and 18% in Japan. There was little serious cost inflation in chemicals during the period, and the rates represented real growth for the most part.

Employment on the other hand remained remarkably stable and showed a slow declining rate of increase. The Japaness chemical labour force which expanded quickly between 1958 and 1963, from 293,000 to 385,000, levelled off afterwards, reaching 416,000 in 1968. Average total employment of the eight principal chemical producing countries went from 1,366,000 to 1,646,000 or 21% in the ten-year period, less than an average of 2% a year. Even in the US, where chemical growth has been most marked, total employment rose only from 794,000 in 1963 to 1,003,000 in 1968, or a little over 25%. In 1968 the total chemical labour force of the West rose 0·2%, while Western chemical output increased 11%. For the United States, employment in the industry rose 5% compared to a rise of 9% in production.

Productivity, expressed in terms of value added per person, has consequently outstripped figures in most other branches of industry. In the 1960s, it averaged $7,000. During the latter part of the decade it rose to over $10,000 per person. This reflects an annual growth rate in productivity of around 9%. In the United States it rose to an average of $20,000 per person over a ten-year period, and reached $25,000 per person in 1970, even though its rate of growth is lower—around 5% annually. For Japan, the rate of increase in value added per person has been averaging around 20% during the last five years in the chemical industry as a whole.

This, of course, has meant dramatic falls in unit labour costs in the industry. Although exact figures are hard to come by, the bench mark used of informed management, but seldom admitted publicly, is under 10% (except in the case of benzenoids or dyes where the process is still relatively labour-intensive, and where it is around 20%). Nominal wage increases in the chemical industry have risen at an appreciably faster rate during 1969 and 1970 than during the earlier part of the decade, when productivity gains and price rises moved well ahead of annual wage gains, accounting for the present low unit labour costs of the industry. Such low unit labour costs and exceptionally high added value coefficients makes it very easy to absorb increases in wage rates.

The thirteen British unions representing the workers of ICI submitted a claim to the company in April 1971 for adjustments in wages and a positive employment collective agreement. The brief supporting the claim demonstrates in impressive detail that between 1963 and 1969 home supply prices of chemical industry products (wholesale) rose by 6·4%, of which probably not more than 0·4% could be explained by pay increases. Wages and salaries per unit output in the British chemical industry rose by only 2% between 1963 and 1969, in face of a rise in the wage and salary index of 52·5% during the period. This virtually constant unit labour cost contrasts with a 21% rise in wage and salary costs per unit of output in British industry

TABLE VIII. 4. *Chemicals: Output and Employment, 1963–1970*

1963 = 100

	Output (Index)	*Employment (Index)*	*Productivity (Index)*	*Annual changes*
1965	117·1	101	116	—
1966	123·4	103	120	+3
1967	130·4	101	129	+7½
1968	140·0	99	141	+9
1969	149·2	102	146	+3
1970	(158 to 159)*	102	(155)*	+6*

* Estimate.
Sources: Index of Industrial Production, *Employment and Productivity Gazette*

generally. The following table of output and employment in the British chemicals' industry, as the union brief states, clearly shows that 'the inflation is stemming mainly from outside the chemical industry'.

In Japan, unit labour costs in all manufacturing in 1967 were 2% lower than in 1966, and 1% lower in 1968. They rose in 1969 by only 2%. For the chemical industry, unit labour costs have been falling steadily regardless of the high increases in hourly rates and earnings of 12% to 15%. Including the exceptionally high increases of 1970, unit wage costs in the chemical industry, measured on the basis of 1966 as 100, were 119 in the United States—a rise of less than 5% a year; 107 in France—a rise of about 4% a year; 116 in Italy—about 4% a year; and 113 in Germany—less than 4% a year. These figures of the OECD, when balanced off against consumer and industrial price rises of between 4% and 8%, seriously qualify the hypothesis that wage costs are triggering inflation. The claim is manifestly inapplicable to the chemical industry with its lower unit labour costs and higher investment and productivity ratios compared to manufacturing in general, as the above figures confirm. Price-setting practices, distribution costs and, above all, advertising and capital investment budgets determine price levels in chemicals, not nominal wage increases, regardless of how much higher they may be than in other branches of industry.

This is as valid for chemical wages in the developing countries as it is in the industralized regions. The chemical industry's scale of plans has reached the threshold level where changes in volume have the effect of changes in kind. Not only are installations bigger and more costly, they are different in composition, character and functions, including the entire integrated relationship between wage rates, unit labour costs and prices.

NO WORK, NO WAGES—JUST CAPITAL

The UN Industrial Development Organization (UNIDO), in a

monograph on the chemical industry and industrial development published in 1969, commenting upon the nature of economies of scale, stated:

'The most significant source of economies of scale is the reduction in the cost of fixed investment per unit of annual output as the annual capacity of the plant increases. While there is also a sharp reduction in unit labour requirements in these circumstances, the importance of this factor is relatively minor because labour costs represent in most cases such a small fraction of total production cost, especially with respect to the basic chemicals.

'From the point of view of economic development, it is important to relate economics of scale to the primary factors of production, especially capital and labour. In most developing countries, foreign exchange is of critical importance, not only as an ingredient in capital but also as a continuing requirement for material inputs. As regards capital, which includes working capital for stocks and other purposes, the amount required is generally proportional to fixed investment. It follows that the use of an excessively small scale of production raises the capital-output ratio for the economy as a whole and thus slows economic growth. The risk is particularly great in the chemical industry because, as shown above, the most important source of economies of scale is precisely-fixed investment. This is not the general situation in other industrial sectors; in the metal-transforming industries, for example, production on a small scale or in short series has mainly the effect of increasing labour requirements rather than utilizing capital equipment less efficiently, and this causes a smaller reduction in the growth rate of the economy (assuming that there is a labour surplus).

'In the chemical industry much of the production machinery and equipment has a relatively short life-span and therefore the choice of a high rate of production in order to obtain the economies of scale implies a constant flow of replacement machinery and equipment. Even if manufactured locally, such machinery and equipment may be in short supply; more generally, the supplies have to be imported and impose a severe burden on foreign exchange resources. In either case, the growth of the economy is constrained. In industries where the diseconomies of small-scale production take mainly the form of low labour productivity, the retardation of economic growth will be far less pronounced than in the chemical industry (providing that there is a labour surplus). On the other hand, under conditions of high growth rates, the manpower base is the ultimate limiting factor and all diseconomies of small-scale production will have the effect of retarding growth.'

On the section dealing with employment the report added:

'The chemical industries provide very few jobs, especially for unskilled labour, and therefore contribute little to solving the often very serious problem of under employment in developing countries. Few industrial sectors have lower labour costs in relation to sales than do the chemical industries.

'The point is well illustrated by the estimates of manpower requirements for an ambitious import substitution programme in Latin America derived from an ECLA study of the chemical industry.

On the assumption that production would be concentrated in integrated plants serving the entire regional market of twenty republics, it was estimated that manpower requirements would be 20·3 million man-hours per year, thus providing jobs for about 10,100 people. On the other hand, in the absence of regional integration, the five largest producing countries of the region would require some 49·1 million man-hours per year for their output of the selected chemical products, and this would generate jobs for about 24,600 workers. When it is added that the labour force in Latin America was expected to increase by roughly 2 million people per annum in the mid-1960s, it may be seen that the projected programme was capable of employing between 2½% and 1½% of the *increase* in the labour force of the region which occurs in any single year.

'Compared to other industrial sectors the chemical

industry is a relatively small employer of skilled labour but a relatively high employer of technical and professional manpower.

'An ECLA study found that in Peru skilled labour represented about 15% of total labour in the chemical industry, compared with about 80% for the apparel industry, 50% for furniture, 30% to 40% for textiles and about 25% for metal manufacturers and machinery. A similar picture emerges from a companion ECLA study dealing with Argentina, where the chemical industry employs a smaller percentage (12 to 15) of skilled labour than the seven other industrial sectors analysed.

'In regard to technical and professional manpower, the chemical industry appears at or near the top of the list of industrial sectors in the ECLA studies of Peru and Argentina cited above, together with machinery and transport equipment and, in the case of Argentina, petroleum. As a proportion of total employees the technical and professional group represents 4 to 6% for Peru and 6 to 8% for Argentina.'

Therefore the 'cash-flow effect' applies to the whole chemical industry, including the industrialized and developing economies. For identical reasons, the chronic inflation of 25% to 80% of certain Latin American countries, Indonesia and the African states cannot be attributed to wage costs—especially as the bulk of investment is going into modern capital-intensive operations, where unit labour costs on the basis of the prevailing low nominal rates are of no consideration at all in the modern plants.

PLASTICS—THE BASIC MATERIAL OF THE FUTURE

The super-growth industry of the petrochemical group will, without doubt, be plastics. Twenty years ago it accounted for only 3·8% of total world production, today it accounts for 7·5%, and by 1980 it will reach 15%, doubling every five years. Investment will reach around $200 billion in the decade ahead. Unlike the other two biggest spenders, end products will not be concentrated in large specific plastic firms *per se*. The basic material supplier will be petrochemical and chemical firms, but the fabricators will ramify throughout many branches of industry. A majority of the global enterprises will diversify into plastics as it invades the construction, furniture, paper, and glass industries, and as plastics replace traditional materials such as wood, metal, cement, etc. Steel growth in the 1970s will average 4·7% compared with 15% in plastics. It will be an industry which will develop in both the consumer and capital goods sectors; for both it will require high capital investment and low-cost labour inputs.

It is not easy to predict the percentage increases of various products. However the basic raw materials are intermediate products supplied by the petrochemical industry: ethylene, Propylene, butadiene, benzine, toluene, methane, ammonia and several others. The production of these chemical derivatives of petroleum refining entail large-scale, capital-intensive plants and are largely continuous-process operations with an exceptionally high degree of automation. Polyolefin plants are expected to reach a combined capacity of 30 to 35 million tons a year by 1980; PVC plants, including copolymers, about 25 million tons; and polystyrene plants, perhaps 15 million tons. The one sector of plastic production which has been relatively labour-intensive, using comparatively simple equipment, has been the manufacture of products based on thermosetting-resins. Now even this has become continuous-process, capital-intensive production.

Perhaps the best indicator of the size of investment growth in plastics is the forecast of planned investments in the petrochemical industry. In the US the basic petrochemical intermediates contributed one-third of the tonnage of the chemical industry as a whole and 60% of its value. Today the figure is around 50 million tons of products, having a value of just under $10 billion. The proportions are about the same in most industrialized countries. A United Nations report on the plastics industry forecasts investments in the petrochemical industry as follows:

TABLE VII. 5

	In millions of dollars Period 1965–70	*Period* 1970–5	% *rise*
United States	5210	7280	50
Japan	2280	3700	63
European Economic Community (EEC)	4000	5350	33
European Free Trade Association (EFTA)	1400	2050	46
Latin America	895	1445	61

Depending on the degree of elaboration of the product, investment per unit of capacity increases rapidly. To tranform crude petroleum into petroleum products, approximately $20 per ton per year must be invested. The transformation of ammonia into urea and ammonium sulphate in a fertilizer production complex requires $50 per tone per year. The polymerization and spinning of caprolactam to obtain continuous filaments of fine denier nylon requires $3000 per ton per year.

Looking into the future, to 1980, the automotive industry foresees vast changes in materials and processing techniques used to form the outer shell of cars. Currently-used materials will be replaced by plastics to such a degree that present-day vehicles will appear as obsolete as the first model-'T' Ford by 1980. It is estimated that 200 pounds of plastic per car will be needed so that, assuming an average of 20 million cars per year throughout the world, 4 billion pounds of plastic a year will be needed, which will come to dominate the motor-car industry.

Worldwide plastics demand will triple by 1980 to over 100 million metric tons. It will probably surpass 1500 million tons by the year 2000. *Per capita* consumption in Japan will surpass the US during the decade, even though US *per capita* consumption will double from 101 pounds to 218 pounds. West German consumption will be nearly trebled. Dutch plastic production, now over 1·5 million tons, is doubling every two and a half years compared to every six years in the US.

All of this unprecedented expansion will require correspondingly unprecedented capital investment. The rate of obsolescence of equipment will be very high. Extremely liberal depreciation margins will be required to stay modern and up to date. And high profits are already seen as a must for quick write-offs and reinvestment. Given that plastics were born from the age of science, they have no tradition or past in industry. As the modern younger generations take the computer and automation for granted, so plastics will not be concerned with labour or labour costs, which have never been significant, but with prices, profits and cash flow.

IX. Petroleum International

POLITICS AND PRICES

The petroleum industry is the prototype of what industry will become in the post-industrial era. Its structure, policies and operations do not conform to conventional patterns. In many respects they refute most assumptions on economic behaviour, and violate most political, social and moral standards still assumed to be applicable to corporations. Though more advanced, it is but a forerunner of the industrial system of the 1980s.

Legally independent and largely privately owned, the eight majors (Standard Oil of New Jersey, Standard of California, Shell, BP, Gulf, Texaco, Mobil, and Compagnie française des Petroles) are extensively linked together in consortia—both with one another and jointly with governments. This is especially the case in the Near East with ARAMCO, Iranian Oil Participants, Iraq Petroleum Company, Kuwait Oil Company, Abu Dhabi Marine Oils, etc. Others are jointly owned by governments of different countries. The interlocking ownership of the world's main crude-oil pipelines around the world, the very numerous joint ventures with one another (Shell has such ventures with ten other companies), common ownership of various operations, and the interpenetration of their public and private financial associates, make it impossible to fit the petroleum industry into any classical framework or system for describing economic behaviour. The petroleum companies, by their nature, are the foremost multinational firms in the world with totally integrated global strategies.

When one speaks of petroleum, one is forced to speak of politics. Nationally, the political power of the oil industry in the USA, UK, France, Belgium, or Holland is unrivalled by any other industrial group, and perhaps by any political group as well.

In regard to the producing areas of the Near East, Africa, Latin America, Indonesia, etc., politics are to a large extent, for better or for worse, based upon oil. Oil lies at the bottom of most major political change in these regions, from counter-revolutions to nationalizations, from independence movements to the building of schools and hospitals. Oil politics are extremely 'fluid', able for example to make extraordinary arrangements such as allowing Israeli tankers and pipe-lines to carry Arab oil to the Mediterranean with the full knowledge and tacit agreement of national leaders.

Eight leading Arab oil-producing nations have recently announced their intention to directly enter many phases of the oil business through new multinational companies. The group comprises representatives of the governments of Libya, Kuwait, Saudi Arabia, Abu Dhabi, Algeria, Bahrain, Dubai and Qatar. Last year those countries produced about 12·8 million barrels of oil daily, or more than 25% of the world's supply. They hold proven reserves of about 360 billion barrels, or about 59% of the Free World reserves.

In June 1971 this organization established the Arab Tanker Co., jointly owned by all eight countries. This company expects to begin operating its own oil-tanker fleet. It will also establish, at the same time, General Petroleum Service Co., which will be authorized to engage in joint ventures with foreign companies, either privately owned or state-owned. These ventures will include not only oil exploration and production, but oil-refining and petroleum-product marketing as well.

A third new multinational concern will be a finance corporation. This will raise capital for the other ventures by borrowing from international financial institutions. The ventures will initially have capital from oil tax and royalty revenue of the member countries. And they will get additional financing through the joint-venture agreements made with foreign oil companies.

A spokesman for the countries announced that the petroleum industry is 'at the threshold of a basic structural change', in which the governments of the oil-producing countries will no longer be satisfied with participation only in the producing end of the business. But they stress that the group wants to maintain a suitable climate for investment in oil by private companies.

It is likely, however, that among the most likely to engage in future joint ventures with the new Arab multinational companies will be the state-owned or state-connected oil companies, such as Italy's Ente Nazionale Idrocarburi (EN,); West Germany's Deutsche Erdolversorgungsgesellschaft (Deminex); and Japan Petroleum Development Corp. (Japex).

The Arab group is separate from the ten-nation Organization of Petroleum Exporting Countries, although this includes many of the same countries.

The formation in 1960 of the Organization of Petroleum Exporting Countries (OPEC), signalled a new level of political horse-trading between the highly cartelized companies (who were used to playing countries off against each other) and the oil-producing states. The short-term intent was to make the OPEC a counter-cartel to co-ordinate and harmonize the conflicting interests of its members and keep up prices by protecting them from company dictates and market power. The aim is to raise the part of oil income received by the producing countries, which is only 6% of the price of a gallon of petrol. The long-term goal is to wrest ownership of the industry from the Western foreign companies, without of course losing their US and European markets.

Following upon the generalization of the fifty-fifty profit-sharing agreements in the 1950s, the parallel cartelization of producing countries and the oil corporations has effectively transformed price-setting of oil into a political rather than an economic process. The protagonists are involved in politico-military game plans, from which the conventional economic factors are extremely remote. Consequently the prices of petroleum products derive from political actions, rather than cost-profits considerations.

Modern industrial societies are almost exclusively dependent on energy derived from fossil fuels. The demand for oil, currently about 60% of the total energy consumption in the Western World, will grow between 7% and 10% a year.

Even at 7%, Western Europe will need one billion tons a year in 1980.

The price changes of energy have repercussions throughout the economy, and have a direct impact upon cost of living indexes. This is particularly true for oil, which provides either directly or indirectly, the energy for practically all the transportation in modern society, and thus influences the delivery prices of most commodities. Within the industry itself, transportation costs are an important factor in prices.

Both the costs of supplying crude oil to the refinery, whether by tanker, pipe-line or overland transport, and distributing the refined products to intermediate depots and consumers, are decisive factors in determining scale, location and type of refinery. Also oil prices decisively influence electricity prices and thus costs of utilities, steel aluminium, etc.

Labour costs negligible but prices going up

Compared to these major considerations, the labour cost factor is negligible in determining prices. At all stages of the petroleum process, from prospecting and pumping of crude oil, through processing and distribution of refined products, the unit labour costs have little direct bearing on price levels.

The President of the Oil Workers' Union in the USA claims that total labour costs in a gallon of gasoline do not exceed 2 cents. In chemical intermediates, in which petroleum companies are heavily engaged—such as ethylene, the basic block of many end-products—unit labour costs per ton of output is under 1% in modern refineries.

When the US oil firms reported final sales and net earnings for 1970, they showed generally positive positions. The giant of them all, Standard Oil of New Jersey, posted a 5% net rise to $1·3 billion on revenues of $18·78 billion.

Gulf Oil reported profits up around 10%. The Belgian Petrofina group reported group net income of $61·3 million —up 7%. Italian state-controlled ENI oil group's consolidated sales rose 14·5% to around $2560 million, while net sales were above $1760 million. Investments made during the year amounted to $608 million, or 24% above those of 1969.

A few claimed not to have done so well. Shell, the world's number six, registered a back-fall in the year's earnings, or around 18·5%; and City Service, in the USA, a fall of 6·8% in the 'indicative' net profit figures. But in explaining the reasons for the fall in earnings, the companies cited higher taxes, increased costs of various kinds (especially structural costs), reduced economic activities, but not rising wages, which are no longer credible alibis for price rises.

A recent analysis of price components of a litre of gasoline paid by the consumer in Europe revealed that for Algerian oil, taxes on the consumer were around $40 per ton, for which Algeria received $5 and the French refinery company got $5·60 in profits, including $3 for depreciation.

The cost breakdown of a typical OPEC gallon (imperial) is as follows:

Consumer government taxes	45%
Distribution	22·5%
Producer government's share	12·5%
Transportation	9·0%
Refining	4·5%
Oil company's net return	4·0%
Cost of producing crued	2·5%
Total	100·0%

The actual cost of producing a barrel of oil in the Middle East is only 15 cents, compared with 51 cents in Venezuela and $1·25 in the US. Direct labour costs are inherent in only the distribution, refining and crude production, which together account for 38·5% of the retail price. Labour cost, including maintenance, in a barrel of crude oil is less than 5%. In transport and distribution it is less than 10%, in refining less than 8%. Erring on the side of too high an estimate rather than too low, average unit labour costs in a gallon of petrol could not possibly exceed 6%, and the figure is most likely closer to 4%. This would put total wage costs of a gallon selling for 26·6 cents at around 1·5 cents. Obviously such a low figure (even if it were doubled to 3 cents) has little influence on prices. A 50% rise in wages throughout the process from crude production to the petrol pump would only cost the companies three-quarters of a cent to one cent more per gallon.

EXPERT OPINION

Sir Eric Drake
Chairman of British Petroleum

Sir Eric Drake, Chairman of British Petroleum, said in his annual statement to shareholders in March 1971, referring to the negotiations with Libya and the Gulf countries, that the cost increases involved 'can no longer be absorbed by the industry and must therefore be passed on as quickly as possible to the consumer'.

'This will cause a rise in the cost of energy all over the world,' Sir Eric said. 'But I must remind the consumer that by far the greater part of what he pays for motor spirit, and a large share of what he pays for many other products, consist of taxes on products levied by the governments of consumer countries.'

McFadzean
Managing Director of Royal Dutch/Shell

'A shift in selling prices of one-tenth of a US cent per gallon in a year's operation means a difference in pre-tax income of $80 million a year, up or down. (By such a ratio, one per cent change would mean $800 million either way.) Shell concurs in free world need forecasts for the seventies of 200,000 million barrels, or more than twice as much as the sixties . . . and that the pace of capital spending might have to increase faster than the rate of market growth. With the likely outlay of $300 billion in the seventies (average of $30 billion annually) this enormous capital expenditure required to meet anticipated demand . . . would not be forthcoming if prices were to react for any period of time to the level prevailing several months ago.'

Price-fixing practices abound in the industry. For example, the American companies, through the Gulf basing point system, make American users of Algerian and Libyan crude oil pay 50% more than posted prices in the countries themselves. Actually, much of the current disturbance between the Gulf States and the fifteen companies that produce 80% of OPEC oil accompanies hard bargaining to arrive at a new optimal operating agreement which will permit higher receipts all round through price-setting, rather than through greater production—just as the companies proceed in the USA.

In an interview published in a petrol trade journal, Egypt's Minister, Mohammed Riad, stated: 'I am not asking them [Gulf States with most reserves] to stop pumping. I am not asking them to stop production. I say to them: "Why must you increase your production by 20% annually when you can obtain the same results with an increase of 5% or 6% higher prices?" What counts for us is to control production.'

Petroleum prices are certain to continue to rise during the next decade, as the era of relatively cheap fuel comes to an end. Prices have already risen almost everywhere in 1970. In the UK, prices of petrol and fuel oil rose three times during the year. Prices of heavy fuel in Belgium increased 62% during 1970.

Consequent upon the Tehran agreement between the oil-producing countries and the companies, signed in February 1971, a first price rise of 3 cents per gallon was announced. The new agreement between the twenty oil companies and the producing countries will be costly for consumers. Pressing their advantage, the producing countries of OPEC presented the Western oil companies with a collective demand for a new split in net profits from the 50/50 rate to 55/45 in their favour, and a new 35 cents per barrel rise in the posted prices (the fixed price per barrel upon which royalties and taxes are paid). (Venezuela is at a 60/40 rate.) The oil-producing countries demanded, with justification, a greater share for themselves in the total oil revenues. The agreement, which is to run for five years, has an escalator clause providing a 2·5% annual rise in posted prices to compensate for inflation. The producing countries would receive a supplement of $10 billion dollars during the five-year life of the agreement. For the companies, this represented an increase of 20% in the cost of crude. As the producing countries' share of the barrel is only 12·5%, it would mean a rise of only 2·5%, or about 0·375 cents, per gallon.

However, following the Tehran agreement, negotiations with Libya also led to a separate five-year agreement signed on 3 April, 1971. This provided for an increase in posted prices of around 35%, guarantees against inflation by the application of an escalator clause, and other commitments relative to intensified prospecting and investment. The settlement reached is higher than the Tehran pact by about 15%. Immediately upon the signing, representatives of the OPEC countries announced that they would seek alignment of their agreement with the now favourable terms conceded by the oil companies to Libya. It is absolutely certain that their demands will be met, thus boosting costs to the refiners even further. The net result should be a rise in costs of around 3% (or around 0·5 cents per gallon).

But already the industry is preparing consumers for increases substantially higher than this figure. The reason why the companies need to exploit the highly-publicized agreement to justify exorbitant price increases is clear. The increases provide the means for fulfilling their cash-flow requirements.

The first price increases announced by the companies—of 2 pfennigs a litre in Germany, 5 lire a litre in Italy, 2 pence a gallon in the UK, 3 centimes in Switzerland, and 28 US cents a barrel more in Japan are over ten times the actual costs to the companies; that is, $10 more will go into cash flow for every dollar paid out to the producing countries. It is certainly not being to venturesome to predict that we shall be involved in a period of long and tense controversy between the companies on the one side and between consumers and independent refiners on the other.

EXPERT OPINION

Sir David Barron
President of Royal Dutch/Shell
February 1971

Speaking to the Energy Club in London on the Tehran agreement, Sir David Barron stated that the moment of truth had arrived for consumers of petrol products: 'For the moment there is no doubt that the petrol market has ceased to be a buyer's market dominated by supplies.'

Not only did he indicate that the increase in costs in the Persian Gulf area and Mediterranean area would require a rise in prices for consumers but, 'even when the flow of petroleum has found its normal level, petroleum products will remain scarce on the European market and this scarcity will persist for a much longer period than those which followed the preceding crises in the Near East'. The reason, he said, was that low prices had stimulated demand during the last few years, but they 'reduced the profit margins of the companies to levels which obliged them to reduce their investments. As a result the increase in capital expenditure in 1969 was the lowest recorded in the last six years.'

Mr John Kircheis
Chairman of Mobil Oil

Explaining the industry's capital and investment policy recently in London, Mr Kircheis confirmed that

'the pressures on the economics of the oil industry have increased tremendously over recent years. It is my opinion that these pressures will increase in 1971, particularly in the area of costs.

'Yet the industry has an insatiable appetite for capital. It is estimated that some £100,000 million will have to be invested over the next ten years if the world's increasing demand for petroleum products is to be met.

'The bulk of this money will have to be provided from the

retained earnings of the international oil companies. Generating the required capital in the current economic climate is, however, likely to prove an impossible task without further increase in prices.'

$500 BILLION NEEDED FOR THE SEVENTIES

According to a report by the authoritative Chase Manhattan Bank, the financial agency of many of the important American oil giants, the industry is experiencing a growing shortage of capital funds. It projects the industry's capital needs at well over $500 billion during the seventies—more than double for the last decade.

Despite a growth of over 8% on the Free World demand for oil, the industry's capital outlay in 1969 rose by only 2·7%, from $17·9 billion to $18·4 billion. This marked the smallest annual rise in the past six years, or about one-third of the average growth in the last half of the sixties. On present trends, there will clearly not be enough capital for the industry to meet this target. If companies were to find it out of their present cash flow, at steady or moderately higher prices, the industry would have to achieve an annual growth in net earnings of nearly three times the average rate in the 1960s. If the money were to be found elsewhere, the industry would have to borrow from the capital markets more than six times as much as it did in the sixties.

The result is bound to be a continuing upward adjustment in petroleum prices and 'increasing selectivity in terms of where and *how* capital funds are employed'.

In looking at the figures of capital investment in 1969, the Chase Manhattan survey notes that almost half the increase on the previous year was allocated to transport facilities, while less than one-fifth was applied to production. The amount spent on production in the US was almost twice that spent in the rest of the free world, yet, despite the Alaskan lease sale, it still showed a decline of $175 million on the previous year. Capital outlay in areas outside the US again increased faster than in the US, achieving a 6·8%

growth in 1968 to a total of \$10·2 billion. Total spending in the US fell by 2·1% to a level of \$8·2 billion.

In the field of processing, the industry spent (at nearly \$3 billion) about twice as much outside the US as it did inside the country. Capital expenditures for tankers were increased markedly in all areas, reaching a level of \$2 billion in areas outside the US, although expenditure on pipe-lines fell by \$45 million to \$610 million.

Western Europe remained the scene of the industry's largest capital outlay outside the US, though reductions in spending on pipe-lines and chemical processing led to an overall decline of \$145 million in annual outlay there to \$2·5 billion.

US companies continued to dominate the industry's spending accounting for \$12 billion or 65% of the industry-wide total. Non-US companies, however, raised the rate of spending at a faster rate to a total of \$455 million. American companies spent less in the US (at \$7·5 billion) than in 1968, but more (at \$4·5 billion) in other areas. Non-US groups increased spending both in the US (at \$680 million) and oustide it (at \$5·7 billion). US companies accounted for 81% of the expenditure on oil exploration.

At the end of 1968 the industry's gross investment in fixed assets totalled \$192 billion, a rise of \$12·7 billion on 1967. Of that, \$98 billion was located outside the US and \$93 billion inside it.

Because of a crucial error in estimating the cost of thermal fuels, including the availability of nuclear energy, prices of all forms of fuel have suddenly zoomed upwards. Coal rose by over 50% a ton in the US in 1970. This is bound to be heightened by the costs of pollution control. The demand for new car engines and unleaded gasoline adds another fixed cost factor for which new capital must be found.

The era of rising oil prices seems definitely to have arrived. The enormous need for capital will constitute a continuing drain upon available investment funds, and will make them even scarcer than they have been during the past two years. Price increases to supply planned levels of cash flow for investment will be the major preoccupation of oil management.

In an industry where wages, salaries and labour costs generally, regardless of how high they may go in regard to average general rates, are already insignificant, it will be political, technological and structural changes which will boost prices.

The new pricing and profit-sharing agreements with the oil-producing States would result in minor price increases for consumers if revenue losses alone were considered. They could easily be absorbed in the consumer taxes imposed by governments, who could, in turn, increase profit taxes on the refineries to recover their share of revenue. This is not likely to happen, however.

The new agreements will undoubtedly be used during the five years of their duration to justify exorbitant price increases designed to augment the companies' cash flow and fuel their investments, not only in oil but chemicals, hotels, land development, and so on.

X. Some Economic and Labour Responses to the New Sources of Inflation

REVERSING THE SEQUENCE

Economic policy on inflation has now to be reversed. Under the new circumstances, conventional procedures serve to increase pressures on prices rather than abate them. As we have discussed, this is because fiscal and monetary and incomes policies, though they limit wages and consumption and make capital and credit scarce, do not lead to reduced prices. The resultant decline in sales and in gross income induces corporations to raise prices, rather than lower them, in order to sustain planned levels of cash flow for capital investment. This arises from the fact that price cuts and slightly higher sales do not provide compensating revenues to make up for profit declines.

The same effect follows from the scarcity of bank credits and outside funds. As interest rates rise and credit lines dry up, companies are encouraged to seek greater internal liquidity through upward price adjustments. The net overall effect of fiscal and monetary controls thus becomes self-defeating and the reverse of that which is sought: instead of a fall in demand leading to reduced prices and, by reaction, cutting capital investment, a rise in prices is stimulated with a situation of undiminished capital spending.

The new experience suggests a need for reversing the process. Instead of seeking to dampen prices by deflating the economy, the emphasis should be on reducing obstacles to the growth of retained earnings; lower discount rates and easier money policies would make more external funds available. Higher wages in the key capital-intensive industries which are strongly organized and have relatively low unit labour costs, would help support demand and sales and hence planned levels of cash flow. This would contribute to reducing the aggregate demand upon external funds and help ease the pressures on interest rates and credit. Such a reverse sequence would stimulate the output of consumer goods, and partially absorb the augmented demand in this sector of the economy. At the same time, fuller utilization of capacity would raise productivity and reduce unit labour costs. The net cumulative effect would be to damp the rate of price rises in the consumer goods area and would entail a return to a new partial equilibrium at a more moderate rate of inflation. Absorbing it entirely has become impossible at current levels of capital investment, and creeping rates of inflation will probably be permanent. In fact, the prospects are for a series of inflation plateaux. Price rises will fluctuate within a certain range for a given period, then move to a higher range for another period, i.e. 5% to 7% from 1970 to 1975; 8% to 10% from 1975 to 1980.

EXPERT OPINION

Henry Ford II

Speaking before the press, in December 1970, Mr Ford projected a rise of 3% in real gross national product. 'For 1971 inflation will continue to be a problem,' he said, adding that it will be unrealistic to expect the rise in retail prices to be less than 5%. Unemployment is also expected to remain a serious problem'.

Robert P. Beasly

Executive Vice-president of Firestone Tyre and Rubber Co.

'Why is everybody so concerned?' he asks about inflation. 'It's a way of life. It's a question of being able to have gradual, healthy inflation.'

Harry Warner

President of C. F. Goodrich Rubber Co.

Speaking at a US manufacturing chemists' association in New York, late in November 1970, he declared that 'the federal government should liberalize some of its investment policies so that industry can increase productivity and thus help fight inflation'. Possible ways to do this without hurting profits, he said, include use of economies of scale.

Confederation of British Industry (CBI)

The CBI added a new explicit dimension to the 'inflation syndrome' in its January 1971 position paper to the Conference of the National Economic Development Office (NEDO). Instead of charging that wage increases were pushing up prices, the CBI told the government that 'wage inflation was accelerating a crisis by making less money available for investment'. It stated that 'Britain faces a wave of bankruptcies' as companies were prevented from acquiring needed capital. Even the staff of NEDO fuelled this new concept of wages-investment reciprocal spiral, by alleging that 'many companies have been relying on capital to meet wages'.

The structural revolution means soaring rates of capital investment and cash flow, for direct controls or a new philosophy of economic growth are not on the cards in the foreseeable future. In this context, any economic policy which is to be successful must be highly selective. Qualitatively distinct problems in the different sectors of industry will not respond identically to a wide-spectrum expansionist policy. Their differentiated reactions to the aggregate stimulus will average out at zero or at a very low level.

The question of whether frantic corporate growth is really desirable, or if unplanned growth for growth's sake is not harmful, is just beginning to be posed. Those raising such questions are still considered more than 'unconventional'. And even as the ideas receive gradual acceptance, it will be extremely difficult to transform them into practical policies.

Therefore the most reasonable expectation is that the 'planned capital needs' of the world's giant corporations will continue rising by between 10% and 25% annually. If rising gross profits and high levels of retained earnings are not provided out of growing sales, they will be achieved through excessive price rises and growing pressure upon cost of living indices.

Far-reaching structural reforms of the American economic system—an indispensable precursor to substantial changes in other economies of the West—and the introduction of democratic economic planning and co-ordination of world capital investment are urgently needed. But the probability of achieving even a minor degree of such planning and co-ordination in the context of the present political and economic structure is discouragingly remote.

What is needed at a minimum is to redirect investment to capacity growth, and reverse the present emphasis on modernization to reduce labour costs. A more rational and balanced global approach to direct foreign investment is also imperative. But this also seems impossible to attain under present political circumstances, where the declining power of nation states and governments is balanced by a concomitant rise in multinational corporate strength and mobility.

Above all, governments must awaken out of their hypnotic obsession with ineffectual wages and incomes policies, based upon the fallacy that wage costs are the root cause of inflation. Admittedly, this is not a very comfortable proposition for political officials, who are supposedly custodians of the common interest. But retraining wages in the high-productivity, capital-intensive sectors will aggravate rather than mitigate the pressure on prices as well as inhibit the evolution of reasonably effective systems of industrial relations.

LEVELLING WAGES WILL SHARPEN CONFLICT

For workers and the trade unions, the problem of how to deal with wage differentials between the high and low profitability industries is a very difficult one. It has become an explosive issue even in the socialist economies of Eastern Europe which function through central planning and comprehensive incomes policies. How to relate the wages of miners or textile workers to chemical and pharmaceutical workers is as baffling a problem for the Yugoslavs and the Soviets as it is for the unions of the USA and UK. However, in neither system is the answer simply to reduce the differentials of workers' incomes across the board by restraining the higher rates. This has already proved politically unworkable and economically disruptive.

Recent work stoppages and unofficial 'wild cat' strikes in Poland, Yugoslavia, Sweden, Germany, Belgium, Switzerland, Holland, United Kingdom, Italy, and elsewhere, emphasize the growing opposition to centralized union authority and policies. By their nature, the national centres, like national governments, are best (perhaps uniquely) suited to deal with problems in the marginal areas of the lowest paid, least trained and poorest organized. For this reason, they tend to emphasize narrowing of the gap between the highest and lowest paid categories and raising of millions of working poor up into the middle-income brackets. This is an aim upon which there is universal agreement in principle and much sanctimonious moralizing. Practice is another thing entirely. In an economy which is disaggregating and in which challenges to central authority are being mounted everywhere, the levelling precept runs counter to the current of social change.

No particular group really believes—usually with justification—that sacrificing wages on its part is really going to help anyone else, least of all the lower categories. Official appeals for solidarity are always vague as to how the sacrifice of the better off is to be given to the less fortunate. As long as the firm, plant or industy remains the basic unit of the economy in which most of the wealth and decision-making power of society is centred, workers must seek to maximize their share of national revenue in terms of such units. This explains why most of the unofficial strikes in Sweden, Germany and Belgium, for instance, the heightened militancy in Italy, and the rejection of contracts in the USA and elsewhere, were provoked by the highest paid workers rather than by the lowest. The revolt in the shipyards of Poland was a revolt of the better-off workers in the economy, and the strongest and most stubborn opposition to the Czech repression is located in the best paid chemical and metal industries.

EXPERT OPINION

Mr Piotr Saraoszewicz
Prime Minister of Poland

'The country has need of wise reforms to change its system of management, but they cannot be applied in haste without prior analyses and consultation.

'We must put an end to the policy following during the past years which consisted of producing only for the sake of producing. Such a policy is only a waste of work. Stocks accumulated senselessly.'

Yugoslav trade unions reject government policy

In what must be surely a 'first' in history, the Yugoslav trade unions rejected the government's stabilization policy introduced in November 1970 to contain inflation, which was running at a rate of 12% for the first ten months of that year. In open defiance of official policy, the Executive Board of the Confederation refuted the traditionalism of the government, which held that the inflation arose from too high personal incomes. They countered that it was particularly caused by exaggerated budget spending and investments. This is the first time that an official trade union organization in Eastern Europe has formally contradicted the official economic policy of the government in a socialist country and taken the economic planners so aggresively to task.

Writing in its official publication, the Yugoslav Confederation stated that its conflict with the government arose out of the attempt to limit personal revenues:

'The trade unions agreed with the Government that the basic causes of inflation should be sought in the imbalance between the level of national income and spending, namely the notable excesses in the sphere of government and investment spending. Dissension was noted at that time, already, in assessing whether consumer spending and in that context the productivity, of workers was a cause of inflation.

'The government programmers of stabilization measures immediately began preparing the Law on the Freezing of Personal Incomes, as they considered that personal incomes were increasing faster than productivity, or in other words that a share of accumulation was being drained off into personal incomes.

'This view was opposed by the trade unions which argued that real personal incomes are closely following the growth of productivity and that consequently the self-managers are acting in comformity with the principle adopted, namely, that personal incomes shall increase proportionately to the growth of productivity. If anyone can be said to have acted incorrectly, then it is the Federal Government, the Government of the Republic and the communes who still have a very large say in the domain of budget and investment spending.

'In November, and right up to the end of December, the Government did not dare appear in Parliament with the proposal to freeze personal incomes without the consent of the trade unions. It so happened, however, that the Chambers of the Federal Assembly and the Council of the Trade Union Confederation convened simultaneously on December 28th. Mitja Ribicic, President of the Federal Executive Council, and two other government members attended the session of the Trade Union Council. At the beginning of the session, the Council members were informed that the government proposal on the freezing of personal incomes was already being examined in Parliament.

'Although the Prime Minister sought to justify the government measure and defend the proposed Law on the Freezing of Personal Incomes by a volley of arguments, the members of the supreme Yugoslav Trade Union body rejected the government proposal and demanded its immediate withdrawal. It was too late, however, the respective proposal having already been passed by the Assembly.

'The trade unions protested against this act which they

considered a breach of the rules of fair play on the part of the Government. The Council issued a statement in which it is stated *inter alia* "that so important a problem ought not to have been placed on the agenda of the Federal Assembly and the respective law adopted before agreement on the matter had reached between all factors concerned, particularly the trade unions".

'Let it be said that the Law on the Freezing of Incomes will be valid three months at most. Its validity on the territory of the individual republic will cease automatically as soon as a Law on Autonomous Compacts on the Acquisition and Distribution of Income is enacted and concrete agreements reached on the subject. The trade unions will be a signatory to these compacts.

'After this case when all concerned were confronted by an "accomplished fact" on the part of the Government, the changes required in the system of decision-making in the Federal Parliament and other representative bodies so as to provide better guarantees to the trade unions, so as to be able to struggle more effectively for the workers' interests, are receiving serious consideration in Parliament.

'Those workers whose earnings are too low to meet rising prices and the increased cost of living are hardest hit by the personal income freeze. The trade unions therefore consider it incumbent on the Government to do everything possible within the framework of its perogatives to maintain stability in the sphere of prices and of the cost of living.'

WAGES AND PENSIONS REQUIRE ESCALATORS

The economic system provides few people existing on earned incomes alone with adequate security. And, paradoxically, it is often the higher paid workers in the rapidly-changing, science-based industries who feel most acutely the overhanging threat of technological unemployment and professional obsolescence. In the prevailing conditions of today, it will not be possible to effect a cut-off or freeze of higher wage rates without the risk of very serious industrial conflict.

Dealing effectively and equitably with the earned incomes of those employed in the less capital-intensive industries will not be achieved through levelling but through complementary publicly-supported schemes of one form or another: tax concessions, social insurance payments, special wage premiums for low-productivity industries, etc. The time is fast approaching when exceptionally high wages will have to be offered in order to recruit people to do many of the low-status, uninteresting tasks which still need to be done. Garbage collection, sanitation services, and a host of other jobs—just *because* they are scaled as menial and inferior—will have to carry wage rates and a special premium which will be the equivalent of higher-status jobs. Otherwise, the needed services will not get done. This and other variants of upward-levelling will certainly come about. They will be the vehicles for resolving the differential problem, not by downward-levelling through restraint at the higher levels of income.

Business has long learned to live, even profitably, with inflation. All of the multinational companies operating in the endemic inflation belts in Latin America or Asia cope with it successfully, as evidenced by their continued presence and expanding capital assets. Besides the banking profession, which posted its highest returns on assets in history in inflationary 1970, the world's largest corporations generally achieve growth rates in assets and sales which are superior to the rate of price rises in the economy during prolonged periods of inflation. Capital income securities such as bonds and other fixed interest yields are extensively covered against losses through compensation premiums for inflation. During periods of rising prices, capital equipment suppliers and contractors nearly always quote figures which include provisions for anticipated increases in prices. The proposal to incorporate escalation clauses into shipbuilding contracts on an international basis was raised at a meeting of the West European shipbuilders and the shipbuilders of Japan, at a meeting in Hamburg early in 1971. The outlook is for its eventual introduction. Long-term Eurobond issues, placed in 1970 for the first time, provided quarterly adjustments in interest rates for both inflation and international rises in interest paid by comparable securities. In July 1970, Philips, the Dutch electrical giant, signed an agreement with a syndicate of fifty international banks for a $250 million five-year loan. The interest rate for the loan is variable and may be determined for a period of three to six months at Philips' option at a higher-than-market rate.

At the other end of the scale, inflation does not seem to harm the poor as much as is generally assumed. A study prepared by the University of Wisconsin's Institute for Research on Poverty found that in the circumstances of the new inflation, with its particular sensitivity to the service sector, many important items in the consumption patterns of lower income groups do not rise as much as the general cost of living index. The wages of workers in strongly organized industries, especially in capital-intensive industries, are managing to catch up and stay abreast of prices. So inflation is not really as harmful or as destructive as is claimed. Certainly the over-reactive, anti-inflation measures being propounded by our contemporary archaics, seeking to put wages in quarantine, do much more harm to the economy than the ailment they are purporting to cure. It is equally evident that it is not rising prices which are causing the growing unemployment. Despite extensive and continuing effort, no convincing statistical case has been made in support of the thesis that unemployment is caused by excessive wage rises.

General agreement does prevail, however, that those living on pensions, retirees with no secondary sources of income, are the real victims of inflation. The elderly are perhaps the unique sufferers from the process. This finding was the result of exhaustive research by the US National Bureau of Economic Research into what the net gains and losses of inflation were for the different categories of the American population. It found that, on balance, no economically active group—whether in farming or production, whether they lived on capital gains or on earned incomes—

really had a net loss. Only the elderly, condemned to existing on frozen and totally inadequate pensions, had this invidious distinction. Eliminating this immoral anomaly is undoubtedly a top-priority obligation of society. But it has been evident for decades that retirees are cruelly discriminated against by inflation. The standard situation is for Ministers of Finance to bemoan the fate of the pensioners when calling upon workers to forego legitimate wage demands, and charge that it is in the greed of organized labour which is impoverishing the elderly.

However, when it comes to increasing national pension schemes directly, the country's finances always seem unable to afford it. Demands to tie pensions to cost-of-living escalator provisions elicits an equally hypocritical reply that such automatic compensation for price increases would aggravate inflation even more. Nevertheless, there is no other way of protecting pensions against inflation except by automatically adjusting them for rises in the cost of living. Attempts to protect pensions against inflation by freezing wages are fatuous and totally ineffectual, and well as being deceitful.

There is no doubt that a generalized trade-union demand will develop for automatic escalation clauses adjusting wage rates to rises in the cost of living. Such provisions are already extensively contained in collective agreements in Canada, USA, Belgium, Holland, Italy, Australia, Sweden and the other Nordic countries. At the beginning of 1971, 3 million workers were covered by cost-of-living provisions in the US. New drives are developing in France, UK, Austria, Germany and elsewhere to establish similar measures. This is the most evident and immediate means for protecting real wages against price erosion in our era of permanent inflation. It seems certain to spread around the world and to become a feature of most trade-union collective agreements with employers, before the end of the decade. The movement will impel governments to provide public service employees with comparable protection, a trend already noticeable in recent measures adopted in the USA, UK, and France.

EXPERT OPINION

Lee A. Iacocca
President of Ford Motor Company

In a press interview given in Geneva on the occasion of the 1971 International Automobile Show, Mr Iacocca said: 'It takes three and a half years to bring out a new model of car and one cannot shorten this period except through enormous investments which finally the car owner has to pay off.'

Asked whether he foresaw price increases, he stated: 'The Ford Pinto costs $1919 which keeps it within the price range limit of $2000. In America, it is not aimed at the usual Ford market but rather for those who buy smaller imported cars. Therefore, the price has to be competitive. Special bumpers, anti-pollution attachments, security fixtures, such as the air cushion, represents an increase in price of $300 to $600. Add to this $500 for inflation and by 1975 the price of the Pinto will be up to $3000. Since everybody is in the same situation, this applies to all makes, American and imported models.'

This would mean a total price increase of 56% during a four-year period or an average annual increase of 14%. In comparison, unit wage costs are not likely to increase by more than 12 to 14% even assuming that total nominal increases rise by 60%.

Necessary as they are, escalator schemes are not sufficient alone to ensure equity for earned incomes in the inflation decade of the seventies. A new dimension of wealth formation and ownership has arisen out of the cash-flow tidal wave. It has engulfed industrial society and profoundly changed the answers to such historically-frustrating problems as how to ensure justice and equality in the possession and distribution of wealth.

Unquestionably, consumer demands, consumer credit expansion, government expenditures both for defence and social services, improved quality of life amid a cleansed or habitable environment, all will exercise a pressure on prices and contribute to inflation. The dilemma is that only a vastly expanded supply of goods and services can simultaneously reduce their costs and reduce prices, and that this is attainable only through a new dimension in capital spending. But, given that high technology and labour-displacing equipment, which by definition produces structural unemployment, will be the character of the investment, the fall in consumer demand will more than offset the augmented volume of goods, thereby maintaining the pressure on prices.

Effecting the transition from an employment-oriented society to an income-oriented society will be the hallmark of the seventies, and the source of major tensions. Moving from an ethic which holds work to be noble and moral to one in which consumption and output are balanced, will no longer be feasible through full employment and anti-inflation policies, but will necessitate guaranteed incomes and new forms of social compensations. Of course, this will not be a smooth and easy transition. Capital formation on a global scale will be a fundamental part of the dynamics of our political economy. From a national and short-term factor, capital spending has changed into a multinational, multiform, long-term function. It is no longer entirely responsive to transient cyclical adjustments, immediate consumer demand or 'fine tuning' of the rates of interests.

This is the new parametric revolution in the inflation equation of the seventies. Wage costs, consumer demand, excessive expansion of the money supply are undoubtedly influential in raising prices, once inflation is under way. However, they are derivative, not primary or casual factors of the contemporary inflation. They are the symptoms of the condition, not the fundamental cause, which is to be found in the structural changes resulting from the high technology and long-term multinationalism of private capital investment.

ASSET FORMATION FOR WORKERS

Wealth is created today essentially through the growth and concentration of capital assets. It has been projected that by 1985 the hard core of this economic power will be centred in a handful of companies or institutions with an annual turnover of $1000 billion.

In the USA there were 40,000 mergers in 1968. The rate rose by 72% in 1969, and it is estimated at 80% for 1970. These amalgamated giants will employ over one million people each by 1985, or less than a tenth of the industrial work force. But they will control over 80% of the country's corporate assets. In other countries the surge to amalgamation is identical, and gigantism is spreading everywhere.

The distribution of wealth must be redefined. The uneven 'distribution of wealth' is usually taken to mean the uneven 'distribution of income', and raising real incomes is thus deemed to be the route towards social progress. It has been in the area of distribution of incomes that the industrial struggle has taken place.

Even vastly improved social insurance systems, the health and medical programmes and the gradual extension of public intervention and controls in the economy by direct and indirect means, have intrinsically altered this emphasis upon greater equality in incomes. These measures, at least in theory, either effected a transfer in the distribution of national income in favour of the lower categories, or modified the relative distribution of national income according to the dictates of the so-called business cycle. The spread of nationalization and public ownership of industries have also been measures designed ultimately to help achieve a fairer distribution in the national income.

The last decade's focus on growth made capital investment the central aim of policy. Other considerations in regard to levels of consumption, foreign-trade balances, wages and prices, social policy, etc., have been subordinated to this primary objective. Measures to control inflation or protect exchange rates, for example, are still carried out in such a way as to avoid reducing the propensity to invest.

Modern wealth is capital assets

Thus both public and private policy explicitly aim at greater capital accumulation, which is assumed to be the prerequisite for economic prosperity, full employment and rising living standards.

The result is that capital formation is the fastest-rising index in the economy, outstripping all the others, including wages. It has led to unbridled concentration of enormous capital assets. The assets of General Motors, for example, are greater than the national budgets of many countries. The age-old warning that excessive economic power leads to political authoritarianism has never appeared more true, as the suppression of democratic liberties in more and more countries confirms.

The deliberately propogated ideology of 'people's capitalism' is a myth. This is clear when one examines seriously the extent of stock ownership in the United States—the source of much of the literature on 'people's capitalism'—as we have discussed earlier in this book. The term is largely a public-relations device to justify the uneconomic and anti-social function of the speculative stock exchanges, mutual funds and related devices for making the capital-owning rich richer and the earned-income groups poorer. Despite the claim that nearly 20 million people own stocks in the United States, quantitatively they own only an insignificant part of the total value of capital assets. This derives from the fact that issuance of new corporate stocks is only a negligible part of investment in new plant and equipment.

Despite the high rate of inflation in 1970, not a single important Japanese firm failed to increase sales, production and investments. The largest European and Japanese industrial companies all increased their fixed assets at rising rates—an indicator of surging cash flows.

This represents a form of forced or involuntary savings by the workers of which they do not receive their share.

And it promises to be the cause of much insecurity and hardship as the ratio of capital accumulation to earned incomes grows.

The Unpaid Sacrifice

In collective bargaining, management will fight escalation clauses in contracts, even preferring to concede a percentage or two higher wage rises instead. This will make it tougher for workers just to keep abreast. And in the medium term, at least, there will be greater pressure from governments on unions to be 'responsible' and 'reasonable' in the amount of wage increases demanded in the cause of 'fighting inflation.'

Such macro and aggregate policies have long since been a major source of economic injustice. In the name of protecting the purchasing power of money, or the exports and investments of a country, workers have been singled out to sacrifice nominal wage rises. The arguments used seldom relate to what a firm can pay or to its earnings, but concern themselves with national responsibility and economic patriotism. But the enterprise has never been required to make comparable sacrifices. 'Price restraint' is in practice a euphemism. Prices are always maximized in administered pricing systems in one of many different ways. Holding back or not raising dividends is another shibboleth. Dividends are merely deferred and paid later or, as most major stockholders prefer, ploughed back into the firm and reflected in higher stock prices. But when workers forego wage and salary increases, they are lost for ever. The net result is that the firm benefits from the sacrifices of workers' incomes in the form of augmented cash flow for self-financing.

Aims of asset formation

The notion of asset formation or the creation of equity and savings for workers in the accumulated assets of industry has arisen as a logical consequence of such imbalance in the ownership of industrial wealth. Earned incomes alone, no matter how much they rise, cannot provide adequate margins for savings and still support decent standards of living. In a period of growing crisis, turbulence and change, the need for security, for guarantees against dislocation and personal misfortune is becoming more intense. Even the relatively best paid and most skilled can no longer be certain that they will not suddenly lose their skills, jobs or work places more than once in a career. Guarantees of income, better severance pay, unemployment insurances, etc., are all needed; but these are in the main palliatives to mitigate the hardships. Asset formation may be a significant step towards finding a cure.

Summarily, the problems to which asset formation addresses itself are the following:

1. To transform the principle of social justice to include both equality of income and equality in the ownership of wealth.
2. To create a method of ensuring workers' equity in the growth of firm's capital assets and net worth, particularly in periods of price inflation where legitimate wage increases are less than what the industry and corporations can and should pay.
3. Through appropriate social funds, certificates of participation, venture funds, etc., to build up capital savings for workers in order to provide material security, guarantees and protection against loss, diminution and suspension of income. This method would constitute a reserve of purchasing power to help reflate the economy out of a recession when needed.
4. Politically to confront the threat to democratic processes posed by the unprecedented rise in the concentration of ownership of capital assets, which governments and political policy, usually the slowest and most recalcitrant to change, cannot carry out alone.
5. Socially to strengthen the campaign for industrial democracy and participation by workers in the decision-making process, through sharing in the power which ownership of the assets confers on management.
6. Economically to create a needed complement to negotia-

tion of wages and earned incomes in the form of workers' share in the residual cash flow devoted to self-financing consistent with the new demands of our rapidly-changing economic system.

EXPERT OPINION

Herbert P. Patterson
Director of Chase Manhattan Bank

To a meeting of European business men in London on March 12, 1971, Mr Patterson advocated the creation of 'compulsory savings' as a means of fighting against inflation.

'All increases in wages, salaries, dividends, or all other incomes over a certain percentage would be automatically placed into a savings fund.' Such a fund would, according to Mr Patterson reduce the inducement to seek excessive wage increases and furnish a new source of capital for investments of public interest.

Herr Dr Tacke
President of Siemens AG

Presenting the results for fiscal year 1969–70, Dr Tacke, President of Siemens. the ninth largest non-US firm in the world, declared that the group's turnover increased 22% to 12·6 billion marks ($3·9 billion) of which 40% was done abroad. 'With a volume of orders attaining 15·5 billion marks (+13%) for the consolidated companies and 5·5 billion marks for the non-consolidated companies, we have achieved a size comparable to the giants of the US and Japan.'

In ten years Siemens tripled its size. 'Our leap ahead of 22% in 1970 was not realized through the purchase of new capacities but by our own expansion.' During the year, Siemens invested 1 billion marks (18% of sales), of which 200 million were spent abroad. In addition, 842 million marks were spent on research and development. 'The financing was almost entirely assured by the company's own means.' For 1971, 900 million new investments are planned. Fiscal year 1969–70 was characterized by an abnormal rise in salary and social changes which had repercussions on the results. Thus net profit fell 16%, attaining only 213 million marks ($54 million). 'Nevertheless cash flow rose from 8·2 % to 8·4% of sales, or 1063 million marks.'

RECENT SCHEMES

National approaches and preferences differ in many aspects. This is inevitable, and understandable. It is not necessarily a bad thing, for only if programmes conform to the reality of the different economic, social and political situations will they possess the needed flexibility to succeed.

The term 'asset formation' is perforce a generic one, covering a number of differing schemes. At the moment, the greatest interest in such schemes is being shown in Europe, notably in Italy, Germany, France and Holland. However, it is starting to generate interest outside of Europe, for example in the United States and Latin America.

In Italy, proposals have been formulated by one trade union confederation for 'contracted savings'. The plan proposed setting aside by negotiated agreements between the unions and employers a percentage of a wage increases which would be paid into a national fund by employers. Workers would receive savings certificates not refundable before a certain time. The unions would participate in the administration of the fund which would be turned into an investment fund for socially desirable investments—regional development, for example. Although initially designed as an anti-inflation policy to siphon off excessive effective demand, the proposal has been modified into a broader social and economic programme.

Dutch unions have issued proposals containing schemes for building up assets additional to wage increases. One is for sharing in capital growth through workers receiving a share in 'surplus profits' after all costs and expenses including depreciation and dividends have been deducted. A possible basis suggested was that such surplus should be allocated in the same proportion as labour costs to total value added of the enterprise or industry concerned. The second scheme provided for investment pay, additional to direct wage increases, which would be used for necessary 'social investment'. The organizations pointed out that the two approaches were necessarily alternatives, but supplementary, to each other. Capital-sharing, for example, could be applied to larger private companies and investment pay to smaller ones or to the non-profit public sector.

German unions are already negotiating asset-formation agreements for members. Besides the security of savings, the aim is to promote a more equable distribution of wealth by building up shares on the accumulated assets of industry alongside and not in place of wages. During 1969 and 1970 the first collectively-bargained savings plans were negotiated, financed entirely by employers.

Advances such as were made in certain parts of the chemical industry in 1969 and the agreement for the metal industry which became effective in July 1970, have extended workers' asset formation to nearly 8 million workers. In most cases the unions have been successful in forcing employers to admit that savings formation must be granted entirely outside and on top of regular wage rises, and that it is not to figure in the next round of regular wage negotiations. For each union-member the scheme means a total accumulation during six years of around DM 3300—including interest and tax bonus. Many shortcomings still require to be ironed out, and the total annual amount augmented in further negotiations. Some employers in Germany are trying to have the savings negotiated as part of the offer for wage settlements, thereby turning it back into a profit-sharing scheme, with its costs to them recovered through price rises. When this happens the proposals are rejected by the unions.

With these agreements on asset formation, or capital saving, or investment wages, a new instrument is added by the union to its bargaining power which opens up a new frontier for redressing the injustice caused by the concentration of wealth.

Initiated by de Gaulle with a great fanfare, propagated by his successor and endorsed by employers, the French plan of 'participation' in the results of the enterprise is philosophically and intentionally the dramatic opposite of asset formation. The basis of the scheme is a voluntary agreement at any level, plant, enterprise or industry, for sharing in the *net* profits. Termed 'super-benefice', this share is calculated after deduction of cash flow and allocation of retained earnings, upon which nearly 90% of private French investment depends. Thus it is merely a modified version of profit sharing, the costs to employers being recovered through the price mechanism. The unions have declared their hostility to the scheme in principle, though they have adopted a strategy of living with it in practice, certain that it will recede in interest and importance in a few years.

Nevertheless, as of April 1970, 4139 agreements were signed covering 2,500,000 workers, about half of the total authorized under the initiating statute. It is noteworthy that over 10% of such agreements are in plants having less than 100 employees. But the most indicative element is that 87% of the 'participation accords' have been concluded with the plant committees, and only about 12% directly with trade unions.

In other countries, also, the crunch of inflation has produced new union proposals for meeting the government's insistence on stepping up excessive consumer demand in other ways than by sacrificing the worker's income. In these cases the inflation syndrome was the exclusive reason for the scheme, unlike the above case where it was merely one aspect of a broader approach to alter the property relations of society. One such scheme is the proposal of the Union Syndicale Suisse (Swiss Trade Union Congress) to the Government that instead of imposing a unilateral tax deposit on exports, 3% of gross wages and salaries paid by employers, should be deposited in a special fund to be used as a secondary support for improving the national pension scheme.

To avert a devaluation of its currency, the Government of Israel worked out a package deal in February 1970 with the

Histadrut to restrain wages, prices and taxes for two years. The pact provides that normal wage increases occurring to workers in existing or new collective agreements are to be paid primarily in the form of government bonds. Employers will match the workers' 'compulsory loans' by investing equivalent sums in government bonds. It was only with the greatest reluctance, and after lengthy vigorous discussions within the Histadrut, that they decided to accept the deal.

Individual share-distribution schemes abound—mostly, of course, among non-unionized companies. Some have become deeply entrenched. In the large retail department stores there are numerous examples of such programmes. In fact, as a general proposition it can be said that where large enterprises are actively and effectively containing efforts to organize their plants (as in IBM, Standard Oil, Union Carbide, Montedison, etc.) an ambitious share-distribution programme is usually in operation. All such schemes are based on some form of profit-sharing, and the distribution is considered as a part of wage increases. Costs are usually deducted from gross profits and recovered through prices.

Undoubtedly the new inflation is bound to favour capital growth and inhibit even reasonable wage increases because of the changing industrial structure of which it is the product, as we have argued throughout. The interest in and demands for asset formation, investment wages, or other variations designed to create workers' shares on the vast accumulated capital assets as a complement to wages, is certain to become a major union claim in these circumstances. Along with escalation clauses to protect nominal wages against price erosion, this will constitute the reply of workers to an inflation which seems to be becoming more and more permanent, despite the use of outmoded techniques to stem its flood. The pressures of inflation upon national economies, and through them upon social programmes, coupled with the global thinking of the big corporations where power increasingly resides, hastens the obsolescence of national political solutions. This, in turn, increases the urgency with which new checks and counter-strategies must be decided and acted upon by those who would have their destinies decided on other grounds than the amoral and antipersonal requirements of international capital operations. As inheritors of the struggle through the mass of the working population, the trade unions must update their analyses and reactions to match the modern shape of industrial activity. Only through such co-ordinated action at all levels of organization can the technological and economic forces now unleashed be harnessed to serve the needs of those they would otherwise place in jeopardy.

Appendix. Some Examples of Production Costs in Modern Scale Petrochemical Installations

Ethylbenzene production costs

£/ton ethylbenzene (alkar process)

	Plant capacity ethylbenzene	*Ton/year*
	25,000	100,000
Raw materials		
benzene	22·2	22·2
ethylene	8·0	8·0
Catalyst and chemicals	0·7	0·7
Utilities	1·0	0·8
Operating labour and supervision	0·8	0·2
Maintenance	0·4	0·2
Overheads	1·2	0·4
Depreciation and interest	2·2	1·0
Total costs £/ton	36·5	33·5
% of labour costs in total manufacturing costs	0·02	0·007

Acetylene/Ethylene by HTP 15 US cents/Kg.

Plant capacity 330,000,000 lb. acetylene and ethylene
Capital Cost $26,300,000 US

Fixed costs	
Depreciation, interest, taxes, insurance, etc.	2496
Raw materials	3786
Utilities	1490
Other direct costs	838
Labour and Supervision	227
Final manufacturing cost	8837
% of labour costs in total manufacturing costs	0·03

100,000 ton/year vinyl chloride plant costing £2·8 million

	Cost £/per ton
Raw materials	
naphta	7·52
chlorine (cell gas)	11·16
oxygen	2·53
Chemicals	3·36
Utilities	
steam	4·34
power	1·45
refrigeration	1·17
cooling water	1·40
fuel	0·40
Labour	0·42
Fixed costs (21 %)	5·88
Netbacks	
offgas	—0·31
liquid hydrocarbon	—0·38
Total manufacturing cost	38·94
% of labour costs in total manufacturing costs	0·01

For Product Safety Concerns and Information please contact our EU representative GPSR@taylorandfrancis.com
Taylor & Francis Verlag GmbH, Kaufingerstraße 24, 80331 München, Germany

www.ingramcontent.com/pod-product-compliance
Ingram Content Group UK Ltd.
Pitfield, Milton Keynes, MK11 3LW, UK
UKHW021955180926
475701UK00003B/45
* 9 7 8 0 4 1 5 8 2 9 2 7 4 *